PRAISE FOR
ROSAMONDE IKSHVÀKU MILLER

Like Rosamonde herself, this collection of her thoughts and writings is heartfelt and unflinchingly honest. While printed words on paper can never replace the warmth and impact of insights shared in person, these written musings come close enough to remind us of the dear friend we have lost.

—Jay Kinney, Publisher of *Gnosis Magazine*

Lecturis Salutem ("Greetings to the Reader")—in Roman times the readers of new books were greeted this way. In this instance, the readers will encounter a great source of insight and inspiration. Rosamonde Miller was a wise woman devoted to things of the sacred. Those who encountered her even once were inspired by her presence, her Gnosis, and her graciousness. We thank her for all she was to us, and what she shall remain to all whose life and consciousness she touched. For some of us, we say to her not an *adieu* but an *au revoir*.

—Stephan A. Hoeller, Bishop of the Ecclesia Gnostica

I had the privilege of knowing Rosamonde for over 20 years. I also had the privilege of concelebrating masses with her in her sanctuary and in mine. She was "incarnated gnosis" whose life was her teaching, even as much as were her "homilies." She lived the Christ life—all the way from Bethlehem to Calvary, from her earliest years, through her personal crucifixion and resurrection.

—Fr. Seán ÓLaire, PhD

MUSINGS OF AN URBAN MYSTIC

ROSAMONDE IKSHVÀKU MILLER

APOCRYPHILE
PRESS

Apocryphile Press
PO Box 255
Hannacroix, NY 12087
www.apocryphilepress.com

Copyright © 2025 by David Miller
Printed in the United States of America
ISBN 978-1-965646-07-6 | paper
ISBN 978-1-965646-08-3 | ePub

The introduction to Chapter 7, "Gnosis" was originally published in *The Allure of Gnosticism*, Robert Segal, ed. (Chicago: Open Court, 1999) and is reprinted by permission of Cricket Media, Inc.

No part of this book may be reproduced, stored in a retrieval system, or transmitted in any form or by any means—electronic, mechanical, photocopy, recording, or otherwise —without written permission of the author and publisher, except for brief quotations in printed reviews.

Please join our mailing list at www.apocryphilepress.com/free. We'll keep you up-to- date on all our new releases, and we'll also send you a FREE BOOK. Visit us today!

CONTENTS

Foreword	vii
1. Heretic...	1
2. God...	5
3. Love...	14
4. Being Human...	20
5. Ego...	32
6. The Seeker...	38
7. Gnosis...	48
8. Gnostic...	64
9. Urban Mystic...	73
10. Wild Gnosis...	83
11. Sanctuary...	87
12. Mary Magdalene...	93
13. Sophia...	100
14. Words...	106
15. Silence...	115
16. A Prayer...	121

FOREWORD

For the past forty-one years I have had the joy of living with the most marvelous human being, my beloved Rosamonde. She was beautiful, brilliant with an immeasurable IQ, fluent in 8 languages, with the most compassionate, loving heart imaginable. She lived a fascinating life—from being born on a ship crossing the Atlantic in the midst of a storm; her imprisonment, brutal torture, and escape from prison while in a Communist country at the age of 16; to being the first woman to be ordained to the priesthood in the modern era; becoming Hierophant of the Holy Order of Mary Magdalene; being consecrated a Gnostic Bishop...to her death in my arms. Though her life and experiences would seem extraordinary to some, to her they seemed of little importance to being enfolded in the embrace of the Eternal.

Her life from the earliest childhood was one of overlapping mystical experience and everyday reality, without any conflict between them. A mystic being someone for whom there is no separation between the ineffable and the mundane. She coined the term "urban mystic" to describe one who lives the life of a mystic while simultaneously living in the midst of the chaos, noise, and distraction of the city. It is a term that describes her better than any other—straddling the worlds, living with one foot in this one and one in the other.

These are some of what I call her "musings"—bits and pieces selected from a variety writings or talks she gave over the years. By "musings" I mean something carefully thought out, like contemplations or reflections, but deeper and more profound. They are not teachings, nor dogma of any type. There is nothing in them to believe or not believe. They are no more than fingers pointing to the stars. If they touch you in some way, if something stirs within you, it is not that something is being imparted to you but merely a part of you waking up to something already within you, something you had forgotten.

Peace and Blessings,
    David Miller

When I began to speak, I was often heard saying "Don't ever, ever let me forget." My mother would hear me and ask who I was talking to. That was my first conscious prayer. I couldn't have told you then, had I had the words, what I under any circumstance could not afford to forget. There are no words for it, except that since the very beginning I have felt a sense of Presence, a love so utterly fulfilling; such an all-encompassing embrace that went even beyond Presence, for then there was no more presence, no division between That and "I," only an awareness of Oneness and of being outside of time. And then I would return from the Oneness, filled with a sense of trust and safety and the lingering taste and flavor of the Divine Beloved, who with his kiss forever stole my heart.

HERETIC...

When I was a little girl, I used to enjoy talking to the Carmelite priests in my parish. They were unusually patient—or I was unusually dense—for I never felt criticism from them, only loving concern. And concern I gave them! I had recently learned of a nightmarish place down below reserved for sinners and created by God, where there was no way out, a place worse than death, for death was not the end for those people. I spent nights full of horror and outrage. I felt that I had to do something, something in which my age and frail humanity were against me. The age-old theological conundrum of a loving, all powerful, all knowing, and omnipresent God hit me with a mighty force as untenable. This was not the God I knew from experience. This was a fake God posing as the real God, because the real God's love was unconditional and all-encompassing. Finally, I came to a solution to deal with the impostor. The next day, full of determination, I went to speak with Father Hilarion, my favorite priest, to make a vow with him as witness.

I told him of the problem, and that while I was just a flawed human, seven years old, and that I could not save everyone, for not even Jesus managed to do that—people still went to hell in spite of his sacrifice—I would vow to renounce eternal life in heaven, for I knew I had not yet committed any mortal sins. (Well, except the sin of adultery, although I was told I had misunderstood its meaning and had already been forgiven of that and resolved to never again adulterate my wine by allowing my parents to cut it with water.)

I vowed I would renounce heaven if it would keep even one soul from being lost. Hell was a scary thought, and I was sure that I would not end up there—at least not yet. What I proposed was that I would die and that would be it. No heaven for me—maybe a few years in purgatory, but that would be alright. Besides, my argument was, heaven would be hell knowing that people were suffering for eternity.

He was horrified and concerned for "my immortal soul," as he put it. He tried to dissuade me and explain how good God was, but I could not get past the issue of hell to my satisfaction. Finally, full of outrage, I stood and cried, "If that's God, I want no part of him!" and fled from the church. He ran after me, and we talked some more. At the end, he threw his hands in the air and said, "You are either the worst kind of heretic—a natural Gnostic—or you are filled with the Holy Spirit, and I would like to find out which." Months later he came to the conclusion that I was indeed a Gnostic heretic, although I still wonder what the verdict was on the Holy Spirit part.

I am always an exile, a troublemaker, a heretic, even a heretic of the Gnostic heretics. My heart is revolutionary and radical, but never rebellious for the sake of rebellion, always in the vanguard against the powers of the world. A daughter of Sophia who occasionally has a single malt scotch, drinks a beer, or smokes a cigar; fully alive, and completely unacceptable by conventional standards; an offshoot of the living God who sweeps all the senses. I have never written a script for you to follow, and I expect nothing from you. If you write one for me, or expect anything from me, you are doomed to disappointment. Projections of saint or demon will never fit into this fully human articulation of the divine. If you wish to approach me, do so in freedom and without expectation, as I approach you.

Spirituality needs a shock. If it does not receive this shock, it becomes complacent. It must be bold, it must change names, evolve rapidly. Maintaining a status quo and an image stops development. I assiduously avoid being labeled as correct, religious, spiritual and respectable. I have purposely laid landmines against the possibility of acquiring certain types of recognition. I abhor images of authority that lead to expectations. Recognition is dangerous to the spirit; it can make a person believe in his or her own public relations image. It determines the individual rather than allowing one to live at the edge. Time deceives us when we identify with our skin avatars. The urban mystic surrenders skin to the Indomitable Spirit, which temporarily permeates, penetrates and eclipses bone, flesh, blood and sinew, as well as their products, thought and emotion.

Like chalices holding the fiery wine that in a sacred act reveals and exposes the hidden presence of the living Christ, these holy vessels are in turn consumed by the fire that holds them until they are no more and dissolve into their origins. Our mortal expressions of flesh are what Divinity needs for its incarnation in order to affect this world and rescue the sparks of light lost in darkness. Once awakened by the fire, these bodies are made holy in the same manner that sacred space is made holy by That to which it is dedicated. The awakened being knows she or he is subversive in nature. By their very presence such beings stir and accelerate the vibratory frequency of life and extract the hidden light in everything they touch. They break the Wheel in consuming time. By their presence, they transubstantiate.

I have often been called a heretic—not because I rebel or defy any established dogma, but because I don't subscribe to any dogma. I think for myself, not through the thoughts and words of others. Also, because I don't look upon any book or religion as authority. My formal education, initiations, ordinations, and consecrations are not what qualified me for what I do. It is the firsthand experience of That Which Is Beyond Thought that has instructed me every step of my life.

GOD...

When I was a little girl, I would go swimming in the ocean. When I was far enough from the shore, I would lay on my back, floating, with eyes partly closed, watching the twirls and grids of light visible through the droplets of sea water dancing on my eyelashes. I would lay with arms extended and surrounded by sun, sky, cloud and sea. My heart would swell as my breathing deepened with the awareness that I was embracing the waters of all the oceans of the world. I was about eight or ten years old at the time. As I hugged the waters that I could not hold, and yet flowed and enfolded me, I felt in turn embraced by the presence of God, immanent in his creation, while simultaneously experiencing God's transcendence. It was a dual consciousness that while I was aware of my physical surroundings and of every sound and sensation, I was also within something beyond and totally Other, wholly transcendent. I can speak of the immanent God, but Its transcendence defies all words and concepts, even memory, for memory exists in time. I can remember knowing God in its transcendence, but I can't speak what that is: only of what it's not. If there is one thing that I have known for sure and that has survived throughout my life is this: God could not escape from me any more than I could escape from God.

All stories should have a beginning, although when mine began is not exactly clear. Since my earliest recollections, from before I ever heard the word God, I can only tell of being carried in the flow of the Mystery without question or resistance. I'm talking about being in my crib, on through my toddler years, while learning to talk and walk and then beginning reading at the age of three.

My God, my God! How you fill every moment of my life. In pain and joy, you remain always present, Oh ineffable, God above God. I don't know you in thought, but I know you intimately in every fiber of my being, deeper than anything I have known in my life. Oh love above God!

My God is the Ineffable God of every creature, by whatever name It is known in their languages.

Ecstasy seizes the soul that has journeyed through the darkness of God, from God to beyond God. We are no more. The Living One is fire in us. Then we return to ordinary consciousness, scoured and inflamed by the touch of the Ineffable One.

Ultimately, only Being can love Being; and it is the Divine Being in us, the Holy Spirit, that responds to the cosmic event of an awakened consciousness. The awakened consciousness needs no defense, no belief, no explanation, no approval, no recognition, and no concern with past or future.

The Beloved exerts His magnet (Her, if you prefer) and irresistibly draws us and pulls us inwardly into the core of Being where there is no division. We partake of this mystery and revel in the ecstasy of seeing ourselves each time for the first time. The recognition of ourselves in Being enhances and sanctifies our humanity. This is the Secret of the Bridal Chamber while in this world. It is not an outward act, but an act of anamnesis, an all-encompassing fusion of Lover and Beloved.

Oh, the vanity of arguments and pontifications about the nature of being! In whatever way you prefer to think of the Ineffable One, whether within or without, personal, impersonal, anthropomorphic, abstract, form or formless, masculine, feminine, genderless or containing both and more; whether conceived as fictional or as existing in fact, makes no difference. Being responds regardless of whatever name and concept we use, depending on what resides in the profundities of our core that bypasses all imaginings and understandings.

God most often suffers from acute amnesia when clothed in form; still, a glimmer of his light shouts from the depths of density, "Look at Me! I'm here!" His longing to be recognized in each other's faces and in every living thing dares us to pierce through layers of conditioning, arrogance, and despair. His voice never ceasing in his call, begging to be awakened.

The first time that I saw His face; the first time that in a fulminating, defining flash of mystical gnosis I found myself in a world more familiar than the one from which the elements of this physical body had been composed—not this world, not the next or the next to the next world or the next one to that one—but another world with a different reality; the first time I saw His face; the first time ageless gnosis permanently imprinted this brain with what this being came knowing; before this person knew she would be classified as a she or even saw herself as "I."

Wherever we start and in whichever direction we go, we always arrive at God. God was where we began and was in every way station we passed in the journey. "Cleave the wood and there you find me; lift up a stone and I am there" (Gospel of Thomas 77).

God manifesting in any type of flesh suffers from amnesia, but only God can remember God. We think it is us, but it is to the divine spark in us that we awaken, activate, and remember through an act of anamnesis, although somewhat different from Plato's definition of the word. That spark doesn't care what names we give that insight and what hairsplitting distinctions we use. There is chaos and confusion outside and stillness and clarity in the inner aperture of the single eye. What are we listening to? Is it to the world, with its many words that by their obscurity pass for clarity and erudition, or to the inner magnet that pulls us beyond all previous understanding? The first brings us to conclusions. Once a conclusion is reached, the door is slammed, and the lock is thrown. We are trapped by what we think we know. The second, offering no assurance, spurs us ever further into the Great Adventure that may take us beyond the edge of the cosmos and into what has never entered into the human mind.

Our human brains don't rest until they find answers, albeit flawed and temporary, to the phenomenon of existence and its myriad psychological implications. We are also creative. We make stories in order to make sense of our perceived realities, whether those stories bear any relation to facts or not, as long as the brain feels that it has made some sense of it all. Perhaps that's why we create a creator god in our own image. That God may be as good and compassionate as we are or as vengeful, cruel, jealous, indifferent, and envious as humans can be. The worst part is that we worship and serve our creations.

I'm not saying that there is not an uncreated Source, but that Source cannot be seen and much less described through ordinary consciousness. Anything said in words can only point to something that a hearer may or may not even intuit. Of that Source we can only speak apophatically, by saying what is not. Perhaps that's what the commandment, "Thou shalt have no other gods before me" and "Thou shalt not bow nor worship them" means. We create gods in our own image, and we worship our creations.

Is God good or evil? That often depends on whether we just won the lottery or on whether we have just lost everything we cared about, including health and freedom. No wonder Yeshua taught not to make treasures on earth where everything is corruptible and perishable.

The nameless God is the same God of many names. The ageless mantra says not "by my God," but "by your God." May we speak of "The One who dwells in the inner depths of every human being."

The word God doesn't even begin to describe that Encounter that annihilates every concept, belief or lore. The rest is just chasing bright shadows, confusing images with Presence. Just as in the myth of Sophia, we take our projections for Reality, mate with them, and give birth to defective offspring that become belief systems and that sometimes turn into ideologies.

In the numinous experience, there are no God or Gods at the level of Being. We experience the presence of specialized gods and goddesses in the manner that our brain interprets the different facets of enlightenment or gnosis. Although many worship the experience of a living presence as a deity, these experiences are to be identified with the seeker and as intimations of their own Buddhahood. In Western language we can say that the luminous presence we see is to be identified with the blossoming of our own Christhood, either with Christ or Sophia.

The symbols of these representations convey meaning beyond words and impact on our daily expression. They act as Gateways through which we might approach a deeper state of mind and even begin to resonate with it. And in resonating with one aspect, we resonate with the whole.

Humans are just one of the many species of animal. The Ineffable spirit appears in its myriad of forms, be it a chimp or a dog, a bat, a bird, or a tree in the visible universe that as a whole, composes the physical body of the Divine.

Too much of religion remains to this day littered with doctrines and claims of exclusivity; ruled by words rather than spirit, where God is a concept and not a living reality. Mine is a God that, having no name, answers to all names; having no books, is intimated in all books; ineffable and untouchable, yet accessible at any time and everywhere.

St. John of the Cross used darkness as a metaphor for God, for the path to God is always dark. God being beyond thought and concepts, It always appears obscure to the intellect for reason cannot comprehend It, even though it tries. The effort of the intellect has given birth to great poetry and art, not by what it explains, but by what it leaves unsaid.

God acts sometimes like a Klingon lover, leaving us wounded and aching for more. And out of those open wounds drips blood mixed with honey.

God as a Father or Mother fails to move me. I don't approach It as a child but as a grownup, even in my childhood. God as friend and lover is something else. The Beloved exerts his magnet—her, if you prefer—and irresistibly draws us and pulls us inwardly into the core of Its being, where there is no division, in which we remain human, and Divinity remains God. We partake of each other's mystery where we revel in Its nature that has never been apart from us. This is the Secret of the Bridal Chamber. It is not an outward act, but an act of anamnesis, an all- encompassing fusion of Lover and Beloved.

God does not need to be praised or worshiped. God yearns to be lived. Animals, plants, and minerals manifest so that Divinity can be incarnate in them. As for humans, the single reason we're born as human beings is that God wants to become human in us. Those who have first-hand experience of the Divine in any tradition discover this to be so, even if it is for a very brief moment at a time.

When we come closer to recognizing that God is within, we begin to see our own ignorance and suffering in the world. We also recognize that the Divine spark within us and the Infinite Source of Light are One. The result translates as compassionate service in humbly allowing this light to be an agent of awakening in this world. We surrender ourselves as bridges to Divine Love. We permit God to be born and thrive in us.

LOVE...

And no experience of Divine Light comes without an explosion of love. It was as if love were a wine-bearer filling the cup of my heart to the brim. I drank of what was poured for me and grew drunk without understanding why. Of course, nothing changed on the outside, and I did not become perfect by cultural standards. Nor could I ever desire to waste time to intellectually dissect it or understand it. But I was forever wounded with that love that can never hate, keep grudges or admit judgments. My only prayer was, "Don't ever let me forget." Let me drink from that wellspring of love until my thirst is quenched. I don't care what happens to me in this world. Love is all I have, all I am, and all I ever want to be.

I'm convinced that while everything ends, love endures and remains a constant in a universe of change and that love is the secret power that moves all things. Too bad that, in humans, ego and its needs are too often confused with love.

Rather than a duality of matter and spirit, let us consider multiple dimensions of one reality. The slightest encounter with that reality overwhelms us in a love and joy that has always been there even in our darkest moments, and it engulfs with its intensity. We discover that it is not the spirit that needs to evolve, but the evolution of the cosmos depends on the awakening of matter as the Mystery of all Mysteries fulfills its destiny through us and through all its articulations.

Our philosophical, esoteric, and religious beliefs don't matter. What matters is the love and compassion that connects us to one another and to other sentient beings.

My beloved reached out, and my soul throbbed with longing. I left comfort behind and sought to follow Him" (Song of Songs 5:6). As the soul becomes electrified by the presence of her Beloved, she is smitten from the top of her head to the tips of her toes. She has recalled her projections and recognized the One whom she has always loved.

So sad watching many friendships being broken because of a difference of opinion. Where is the love? Do people have to break up with friends because they do not perceive reality from the same perspective? I think not. Peace cannot rely on agreement, for few can agree on everything. A commitment to peace demands open minded listening without ulterior motives, insults, condescension or trying to change the other to our point of view; attentive listening rather than preparing our next argument while the other one is talking; compassion, empathy, and respect. It is possible to agree to disagree without imposing our beliefs on others or trying to make the unwilling live according to our will. May we compassionately live with those who are different from us, and who think differently than we do, that we may be closer to achieving peace.

The spiritual fragrance of my many spiritual mentors gathers around me, their voices softly rising in a harmonious choir that envelops me with their warmth and gentle guidance, each voice a unique hue and quality, all blending, rising and falling in a haunting cosmic melody, their power to awaken undiminished by having left this earth, most of them long before this body was born.

Mystical poetry speaks of the Divine Beloved with the closest language we can use: that of love and desire for an earthly lover. Every love song, every song of longing voices the cry for the Beloved, projected outward to another. But deep within there is that longing for something that never changes and never dies. Our earthly falling in love resonates with love of the divine, taking us perilously close to the edge of that abyss where human emotion overwhelms us and explodes within us. But here the comparison and metaphor end; for the presence of the Divine Beloved takes us beyond the territory of even the most deeply intoxicating earthly love, where the Beloved catapults us to an unheard-of place where we are never to climb back, lost in the Beloved, left without will, without why, and without any wish of our own.

At the end of our journey on earth we may look back at a fruitful or wasted life. Fear or love become the measuring rod. Success is not measured by material gain or loss, but by love. We can live a life based on fear or a life that is the product of love. Love and fear cannot coexist in the same manner that darkness disappears when we turn the light on.

I trust in love. No matter what conditions life may bring, I trust in Divine love, for it always finds its way. This is not based on belief, but in trust in what life has shown me and love has taught me without exception. Trust in love. Love in trust.

Love has no opposite. It is not hatred, but fear that is an impediment to love.

Trusting in love brings us to unbidden, unexpected moments of ecstasy and spontaneous sacraments, "leakages" from beyond the veil into this world of form in a holy Sacrament of the Moment.

I have found much beauty and kindness around me—from those that know me and from strangers that I'll never see again. There have been some very rare, horrible exceptions, but those do not become part of the treasure-trove I keep in my heart.

We are born so that every minute part of Being may love and embrace the other. The indivisible Oneness of Being appears in a symphony of form, color, genders, and kingdoms, and in their sleep, see themselves as separate, alien, and in competition with the other. Until they awaken and, suddenly, they see the forgotten God that never stopped whispering Its secret in the other. All of creation sings this story.

If there is a true human, it is not because of race, economic, social status, fame, beauty, education, age, or religion. If there's a trait that makes a person authentic, that trait is love. That trait is compassion—compassion even toward our enemies.

In a fragmented world, God can only reveal himself in a broken manner. We come to heal this fragmentation. It is said that to love someone you need to know them first. Perhaps this is true superficially, but if you want to know God, you need to love first, unconditionally. How can I know you unless I love you unconditionally so that you can be free to reveal who you really are?

The longer I lived, the more I was convinced that Love was the antithesis of control. That love runs against the logic by which people, individuals, and institutions tend to justify their rule over people's minds and bodies. That slavery, war, and oppression of the weak, the stranger, the other, and of anyone could not stand in the face of the reality of Love.

Love for the Divine carries us beyond the territory of our love for an earthly lover, no matter how intoxicating this lover is.

BEING HUMAN...

I went to check Facebook, bored with all its triviality, all its outrage and anger from opposing perspectives, with nothing better to do, because the pain didn't allow me to read or watch a movie on TV. Then, the first thing I saw in my newsfeed was the face of a friend with a big smile having a drink with a friend of his visiting from Belgium. It was full of joy—not the smoke of someone escaping through entertainment and chic food. The camera captured at an unselfconscious moment, the true, genuine joy he was experiencing at that moment.

I often see pictures with many smiles, showing "fun" moments with family and friends or traveling in beautiful places. This was something else. This was an unguarded moment very rarely seen. It hit me while I stared at it. The mystical moment is the moment of something true. I dissolved into tears—tears and sobs of acceptance of whatever comes to me; tears of joy and unplanned, spontaneous, powerful prayers for all sentient beings. Infinite love and peace filled my whole being. The pain is still there, but with a different quality—pain that is not all-consuming, but just an infinitesimal aspect of existence.

The good thing about being an adult is that you can do everything you wanted to do when you were a child. Don't miss this chance. Our bodies grow up, grow old, and we accumulate useful knowledge, although, hopefully, we never leave childhood behind. I am one of the lucky ones who never grew up.

At birth we are dropped into a combat zone. Our mission: to keep brilliant and alive the luminous spark of Light encased in our three-dimensional uniform; to keep our humanity in the midst of fear; to remain compassionate and without judgment; never profiteering from war or engaging in acts of cruelty. Never forget who you were before being born, for you will return to it after you die. We must not only leave this earth with an honorable discharge, but full of medals of heroism above and beyond the call of duty. Never lose the best of your humanity. Never forget who you are.

A sense of humor and a knack for not taking ourselves too seriously are essential for maintaining a relationship with God. St. Teresa of Avila serves as a good model for us. A well-known story about Teresa tells us about a time when she was knocked off her horse and hurt herself in the fall. She turns to God, saying, "Why do you treat me like this?" Later on, while in prayer, she hears God answer, "This is how I treat my friends," to which she responds, "Well, that's why you have so few of them."

Each day for me has been a day of revelation. Since early childhood I had a sense of my life's path, and often had glimpses of it that gave me a sense of reading the pages of a diary I had written at the beginning of time, and was only remembering each day. Each day illuminated a new entry in my life's journal, each new episode coupled with a sense of remembrance, of recognition, as if I had lived it all before.

The human tendency to complicate things, to try to sound wise, spiritual, and sophisticated brings forgetfulness of the basics. Uncertainty and pain hang as a shadow over all with death as the only certainty. Interspersed through life we encounter beauty, love, generosity, and joy. These precious gifts demand to be lived to the fullest without thought of the past or fear of the future. Ultimately, we are born and we die, and worry is a waste of life.

We are all interconnected. More than that, we are inextricably entangled with the rest. What affects one affects the whole. So does our response to it.

"Do to others as you would have done to you." "Forgive those who curse you." "Bless your enemies." These are the words of awakened beings: Love yourself when you are wearing the different faces and personalities that do not recognize you or want you as their own, as flesh of their flesh and blood of their blood. In our uniqueness and differences, we are expressions of One, although we are never the same.

Who is this One who walks around in different forms, wearing different faces, in every permutation of race, culture, religion, language, and sexual expression? Who is this One who peers behind the hijacker that calls itself "I," who has separated itself from its deepest nature? Who is this Mysterious Stranger who looks out behind temporal eyes that have no clue of their true nature? Don't answer to me. Answer to yourself. Know yourself.

We facilitate transformation when we operate beyond our comfort zone. The mind needs stretching beyond capacity, otherwise stagnation sets in. An oversimplified example of this is going to the gym and building muscle mass that replaces harmful body fat.

We are myth makers, poets, and dreamers. Packets of information interacting with each other took the appearance of solidity and physicality that we continue to project onto a screen of perception. Transpersonal dreams became, through observation, our conceptual and physical reality. This does not belong to the individual mind alone, but to our collective minds and dreams. We came from the Light as Light and have projected into the world an image. We are artists who have created a painting of a cosmos and have become trapped inside the images—and nightmares—that our dreams have made.

The place of life is now. Hellish conditions are not hell in the living awareness of Being. We don't need to rage against the black iron prison in order to be free. We don't need countless incarnations as many believe. We breathe in the Holy Spirit, the Great Mother of all since before time began, and inhale the ultimate freedom that is in Her. Freedom is now, freedom regardless of the vicissitudes that this world outwardly brings to us.

Our physical biography carries the sum of all our ancestors, from pre-human times to before the beginning of sentient life on earth, to the dust of the stars and the impetus that gave them birth. Matter sings within us in all its beauty and ugliness and the wildness and splendor of past and future potential forms. Behind, within, and beyond all that we touch shines the fierce, passionate love and Presence of Being that interpenetrates all beyond concept and understanding.

Stereotypes only reflect a personal belief projected to others. I'd rather not assume anything about anyone. In my experience, each person, human and non-human, reveals a cosmos known only to themselves and untranslatable to the rest.

Human beings—what complex creatures we are. We are capable of the most heinous acts as well as the most sublime acts that can guide us for millennia. We have committed and continue to commit the cruelest atrocities in the name of good and under some accepted absurdities, as well as ideologies, and even because of sadistic pleasure. We support these acts by our lack of self-knowledge. Decent human beings can turn into fanatics overnight with encouragement from religious and worldly authorities without realizing what has happened. They usually mean well. Our collective dreaming can lead to extremes that may destroy us. We need to wake up. Let's not fool ourselves in the belief that one race or nationality is better than another. We are all equal in this, only differing in cultural beliefs and practices, that like all psychological conditioning, is a form of robotic programming. Our capacity for self-deception is astounding when we are sure of the conclusions we have reached. No wonder a luminous man prayed for his tormentors by asking that they be forgiven, for they do not know what they do.

We are also capable of the most selfless, altruistic acts, and not only for the sake of humanity. We sacrifice and work hard for the sake of other creatures victimized by our darkest nature. Our capacity for compassion-in-action can amaze the world despite persecution and mockery from others. While clothed in soma, we are worse than we think we are and infinitely better than we think we are.

Gender has never been an issue in my work and in my personal life, although I can't swear as to whether it has been a problem for others. I feel just as comfortable with men as with women, perhaps because I don't think of myself in terms of gender. I love and respect masculinity in the same manner that I do true femininity. I treasure my friendships with men as well as with women. I don't see myself as a woman, but as a spark of the Divine in a human body that was born female and has always been comfortable, nay, thrilled, within its skin. Gender identifications may be useful to operate in the world, but they are absolutely meaningless in the Ultimate reality that we in the West frequently call God.

Bodies of matter may be transitory expressions of Being, but it is nevertheless lovely to hold, enjoy, and behold the All in every physical form through which it manifests.

My favorite qualities in people are compassion, generosity, a sense of humor—even irreverence, and the ability to laugh at oneself. Life is very difficult for those who take themselves too seriously or believe in their own PR.

Humanity has struggled for millennia with the concept of justice. Punishment is not justice, but a cruel caricature that exactly defines revenge, and revenge cuts off access to the soul with its poison. Restorative justice works better, but there are many acts and factors where no restoration is possible. Mercy is essential, not only when restoration is not possible, but at all times. There is a condition that those who recite the Our Father (also called the Lord's Prayer) have set for themselves when they pray: not to be forgiven from their debts and transgressions (which are many in this world of dualities, for we cannot do good without its negative afterimage) until we have forgiven all. We put as a condition for our own freedom that we will be freed to the same degree and manner in which we have forgiven others. We need to give as much mercy as we would like to receive. It is as simple as that. "Forgive our debts in the same manner that we forgive those who owe us."

Forgiveness and mercy are the gifts that we lay at the Divine altar. They return to us for our purification, that we may proceed with clean hearts and minds.

Nothing I write here is ever to be taken as something I want you to believe. Unless my words voice your own direct experience, something that you know but have not put into words, believing in them will not help you. Sometimes they may trigger your own breakthrough, but such a breakthrough would belong to you, not me.

It never ceases to amaze me how people who are looking for something they know is beyond their knowledge immediately reject something new that doesn't fit within their known system of metaphors. It is almost as if they fear to examine anything that may threaten what they already think they know, and often respond with anger or disdain, contradicting their previously stated desire for more. Others just reword it in their own terms that have nothing to do with what they heard, thus sanitizing any new knowledge.

How do I see the world and all its creatures? To approach this, I must use paradoxical terms. I see apertures through which an inbreak of Divinity is constantly possible. Also, as mirrors—mirrors in a carnival, those that to greater and lesser degree distort what they reflect into grotesque shapes. It also appears like a broken mirror, whose shards must be collected and put together so that they can bring a more accurate reflection of the

Presence facing them. In this world, even when all the pieces have been completed like a jigsaw puzzle, they always show the scars of their fracture. It reminds me of the wounds that Yeshua still bore after the resurrection.

Life is full of adventures that range from the mild to the scary, even terrifying. I see it as an adventure tour, a safari that I signed onto before taking physicality on this planet. If we take an adventure tour and don't encounter some serious challenges that, although scary at the moment, we can brag about later when we return home, we would ask for our money back.

It has been my experience that when reality as we have known it finally crashes against truth and utterly crumbles, if we can avoid escaping into insanity or finding new games to keep the dark away, we may find ourselves at the fulcrum of a revolution within us. This moment mandates our total attention, energy, and passion. We must eliminate any expectations—either recollections of the past or speculations about the future. The second we start looking at the past with relief or regret or start wondering about the future, the moment is gone. In that silence of the mind...the Timeless breaks through time and fuses with our soul. The pathless path to gnosis may sometimes be compared to walking a tightrope in the darkness across abyss guided only by the light within the heart, a light brighter than the noonday sun.

Our physical biography carries the sum of all our ancestors, from pre-human times to before the beginning of sentient life on earth, to the dust of the stars and the impetus that gave them birth. Matter sings within us in all its beauty and ugliness and the wildness and splendor of past and future potential of forms. In addition, behind, within, and beyond all that we touch, shines the fierce, passionate love and Presence of Being that interpenetrates all beyond concept and understanding.

Things that are judged as difficult are only so to the degree that we resist them.

We can create concepts about why. We can live in our heads and make stories. However, life is to be discovered by living it and not wasting it looking for a why, whose answers, if we are lucky, will never satisfy. If they ever do, we are truly lost, for then we have been filled with lies and not with life.

Modern spirituality sometimes focuses on well-being. While ecstasy is an essential byproduct of our discovery of gnosis, let's never forget that heroism and sacrifice sets in us the brand of the true human. We can do no other.

Very often, while pointers leading to awakening are given, the listeners are busy thinking of their next "yes but" or rebuttal to what was said. When there's attention, the arrow may be caught in flight and incredible wonders that thought can never understand may reveal themselves to us.

Somehow something magical happens when we abandon ourselves completely into the hands of Divinity. It leaves us changed in a fundamental way. Whatever is happening on the outside, around you, you are able to dwell in an internal environment of total acceptance and love—an environment that transforms our relationship to the outside where nothing can touch that trust and serenity of mind and heart.

Within every person there is an intuitive sense of the transcendent, an inner knowledge that there is more to life than one is ordinarily experiencing, and a yearning to unfold more of that "more." It is this sense of the transcendent that has lit the fires on every altar, built every temple and shrine, made every religion articulate, and supported every prayer through all history. It is the insistent but silent voice of the Supreme Mystery calling to all creatures, at least human creatures, relentlessly urging them to "come closer."

Life is so gorgeous! The mystery is we are not always deliriously happy. Such beauty, such intolerable beauty. There are but two ways to look at the things of this world: as if it were the first time and as if it were the last.

At one point in human evolution there was a choice on the part of humankind to relate to all that is through the intellect rather than from the heart. Suddenly it created an artificial subject/object dichotomy between self and the rest of creation, the rest of the universe. "I am naked," man declares in horror. Man chose to understand the universe instead of being the universe. Man placed himself out of the flow and for man to return to the original oneness, he must do what he fears to do above all else. And that means to go beyond the conceptual, to abandon his cherished image of himself as a distinct and separate entity, to relinquish the hold of the ego.

EGO...

My ego and Self are good friends with each other. My ego is like a well-trained dog that acts on command. Ego is a pampered, faithful friend; so is my body. I love them and care for them so they don't wither and die. They need leisure time. Sometimes I take them to the ego park or the ocean, where ego can run off leash, but always runs back on command. My ego, my soma, and my flesh (sarx) are my faithful companions and I'll care for them until sarx death.

Not many people really want to wake up and become conscious. They just want to trade a disturbing dream into a pleasant one and reassurance that whatever is wrong is not of their doing and that someone else is to blame. Before jumping to judgment or shooting verbal or written bullets, we need to consider, "I might be wrong."

Semantics play a powerful role in communication, especially on words that have different meanings. Take for instance, the word "mystic," the word "gnostic," and that trickiest of all words: "truth." People often appear to be disagreeing when they are using diverging definitions of the same word when in fact, there is no disagreement, just two widely different conversations. Let's be sure that we are not assuming that the other is using the same definition as ours before adding our two cents worth lest we unwittingly equivocate.

When we realize all the games we play to keep the dark away, how we use and have been used by thought, we finally wake up to who we are and the nature of our role on this planet. Not only do we become plugged into a prior Source, but we are able to unwrap the gnosis of a destiny we have always known but didn't know we knew.

Promoting oneself with claims of being enlightened or of having attained to gnosis, or of vaunting one's intelligence, or of anything, doesn't impress. Let your words and actions speak by themselves. A tree is recognized by its fruit. Anyone who has to tell you they are a big deal is not one.

Evil does not just end in the committing of evil acts. It tends to infect everyone and everything it touches, even indirectly by hearsay. For it is not enough to stop those who have hurt others and try to neutralize its harm. The stain spreads in the human breast, poisoning whole systems and making others accept those acts as normal so they imitate them. Their evil perpetuates itself when those affected by them seek revenge in attempting to inflict on the guilty the same evil they had visited on others. Be aware of what your outrage makes of you and where it leads you, lest you become what you hate. None of us are exempt, so be aware of your own hidden potential for harm.

We believe what we see, but what we see depends on what we believe.

The more a person tries to escape, the more trapped and miserable that individual becomes. Another way exists. I call it "the secret way"—secret not because it's hidden, but because it's so obvious that the conditioned mind misses it altogether. Genuine freedom reveals the need to escape as irrelevant. Ultimately, it's not for ourselves or our learning that we have come. Our contract is not for our sakes.

Many people lie, sometimes daily, and usually in insignificant ways. Strangely, it doesn't bother me when they lie to me. It has nothing to do with me and everything to do with their need to modify the image of themselves that they present to the world, sometimes even to the detriment of others if it benefits them, and others for no apparent reason at all. It would be interesting if, for Halloween, these people would try something new for an hour or two and remove the masks they wear all year round and show the original face longing to reveal itself.

It is easier to worship a figure of light than it is to unwrap what the story is telling us and what this figure stands for and is showing us. This is something that we must see and experience for ourselves, for we can only know what we experience directly and not by what another person tells us or by their interpretation. This is different than receiving guidance to the Source, which becomes essential if one is not to be derailed by illusions.

Once the soul begins progressing in love, the ego becomes aware of the pending annihilation of its control over the individual. There is nowhere to rest. This is reminiscent of the Goddess Khali, with skulls hanging at her belt. The skulls are the slain carcasses of the ego. No one can come to her and remain intact. Blindness is lifted and the ego is revealed for what it is. The person is no longer able to do the same old things. Then, a sensation arises as if the world has taken off its mask for the first time and you can see it all, right in front of you. And you remain without illusion or pretense, in awe and tremendous humility. Suddenly, the images and the names and the words are not just symbols. They are relationships that reveal what they previously concealed. Noticed that I didn't say "annihilation of the ego," but that I said "annihilation *of its control* over the individual."

It is not for ourselves or for our benefit that we come to this world—not to have happiness or sorrows or to learn or to expiate sins, but we soon forget and the rescuers become casualties. We can't help but learn a few things as time goes by in the same manner that pain, happiness, tragedy and joy comes to us in a lifetime. We don't learn the same things out of similar experiences. How we interpret what happens to us and how it alters our worldview depends on the individual person's conditioning and background. The sooner we dismiss our self-centered concepts the sooner we wake up, but we need to be awake in order to see this. May you be able to navigate through the challenges of life and may happiness be your lot more often than not, but may none of it divert you from what you came here to do. Freedom cannot depend on what happens to us or on any outside force. Everything is constantly changing as it happens. Since I began writing this, our planet and the whole solar system have been moving through pre-existing space; and even our galaxy is hurtling through space at 2.7 million MPH (4.4 million KPH) even though it feels like we are sitting still. External circumstances are constantly changing. The freedom of gnosis belongs to a different order than the ephemeral peace experienced when most things go according to our wishes or through the illusory safety some derive from having a belief system.

Many people think and say that they want to learn when they only want to be heard and receive corroboration of what they already believe to be true. Knowledge will challenge all perceived notions of truth, so their immediate reaction of talking before thinking is to defend what they already think is true, rather than examining what challenges their preconceived notions.

That a person had an encounter with extraordinary consciousness doesn't necessarily make them a conduit for light. The experience always filters through the ego. What we think of as reality is only something we have crafted by the focusing of our intellect.

Ego rises in a complaining self and it enhances itself by its complaints. Its purpose is to make the self right and to enhance the fiction of "me."

THE SEEKER...

*S*ince my early teens I explored solely on my own; sometimes under the guidance of teachers and initiators, but mostly alone; without authorities, religions or scriptures. With my body, mind, and psyche as my alembic and athanor, I pressed deeper and deeper, until I plunged far into the unknown. Without a frame of reference, I found a knowledge beyond all knowledge and a love beyond love that left me unknowing and that anointed and hollowed me from within, annihilating everything I knew and thought.

Silently and in secret, the seeker's journey may reach the point when the Sought flings open all doors and barriers. The seeking is over, but the journey without end continues through an intimate and direct revealing after another fashion, free of beliefs, concepts and the desire to convince anyone. Outwardly, nothing changes; however, everything has changed.

Over the years, a practical and materialistic society can rob us of the original mystery of childhood. We begin school to learn the ways of the world, to be serious, and if we don't let go of our innocence, the world by force knocks it into unconsciousness. When it does, we find an abyss of emptiness that we can only fill with tears, crying, not knowing why; not knowing that we mourn for a child left for dead lying at its bottom, and that the child is us. Listen to our innocent dead clamoring for resurrection, crying for the breath of life that will bring the child we lost to life again. Awaken now. Resurrect now.

There is a difference between seeking and permitting that which we seek to pull us toward itself like a magnet. In seeking, we enter an endless journey, fraught with obstacles and setbacks, alleviated by a few achievements. But the object of the search is already present, attracting us to itself with its own gravity. The experience is always of today and of this moment provided we do not resist it.

What people unpack for the first time still remains as a seed maturing and working its way out to the light through pre-existing unconscious filters; whether with outright rejection or with various levels and degrees of understanding. That's why it is important to repeat statements at various intervals. Don't give up if the first or tenth arrow has missed the target. At the eleventh you may catch it in flight and see things in a new light. What was once obscure suddenly opens up, and what was clear the first time opens up wider and deeper, and from the pregnancy of earlier union, a new revelation emerges.

What's beyond the gate has always been here. There's nothing to obtain and no place to go. However, not all get what this means, not even intuitively, as long as we take a maze, rather than a labyrinth, to pursue our journey. They both look deceptively similar, but a maze is full of dead ends, perils, and the need to backtrack each time a path ends in a wall. We can get lost for a long time before even realizing that we are lost or that we are in a maze. A labyrinth has many turns, but it is a straight path to the gate, with no dead ends. Once the Way is known, we realize that we were always there and always knew that we were always there, but didn't know what it was that we knew. Once we know it we can never unknow it.

Often seekers find but miss and do not recognize the Sought even when It is staring right back at them. They have ideas and concepts of what the Sought is, but It is none of those things. They are so busy searching, repeating what they think they know and trying to impress others that, in spite of having eyes, they are unable to see. When all beliefs crumble and it suddenly seems like the end of the extraordinary, the tendency for many people is to just stop there, thinking that they have seen the light, but what they have seen is the end of illusions. It is precisely at that point that gnosis becomes possible and that the actual journey begins, although that journey does not involve time. It is important to remember not to replace the old thinking with new illusions.

Teachers and teachings cover a full spectrum ranging from excellent to harmful, but the excellence, effectiveness, and value of a teacher and a teaching rest on the capability, receptivity, and spiritual intelligence of the student. A student who is not ready will miss the most important points and not learn at best and distort and twist the teachings of even the greatest master at worst. A student who is capable, receptive, and ready will make sense of even the most minor hint. Such a student is able to catch the arrow in flight. Study alone is far removed from the mystical experience. We can learn sophisticated images and mythologies from the experiences of others; but once we ourselves have been brushed by the eternal, everything else remains unsatisfying.

Superstition, fear of death, and speculation of what may come after remain to this day present within most religious belief systems. Past and present history attests to the control exerted by religious traditions that prey on those insecurities, which is most of them. No matter how lofty the teaching, there's usually a catch imbedded in most doctrines. Even many called Gnostic. "Seeker, wake up!"

We have been conditioned to think that we must gain something from our journey on earth. We are invited to consider things from different perspectives, to step outside the rails of the train pursuing us and run in the open fields. Perhaps there's nothing to be obtained. Perhaps we come here entrusted with the task of keeping open and unclogged the holes in the flute that are these bodies so that Christ's breath may freely flow through. We come to do that under any manner of condition, in joy and adversity, in sickness and in health, so that through each of us the revealed may reveal the Revealer.

Sometimes the seeker is so busy asking the questions or listening to their own voices, that they can't hear the answer they sought. They tend to speak before having understood the pointers to what they have asked before.

What prompts a person to pursue a spiritual journey? For some of us we can't see its beginning, since we can't remember a time when it was not there. We don't know all the reasons that propel us on a spiritual journey but somehow our life compels us to go. Something in us knows that we are not just here to toil at our work, or to follow society's dictates. There is a mysterious pull to remember.

We seek spiritual teachings. We shop, and if we find some resonant teachings, we explore them for a while. In our culture we are used to taking those resonant bits from many cultures and trying to interpret them, to fit them with what we have already heard and thought we already knew. We , when in fact we have grown intellectually. At each step of acquisition, we have been able to make some re-interpretations, making greater circles around the millstone. We think we have gone forward in a spiral, rather than just walked many miles in a circle.

Blessed are the events and the people that have brought us misfortune—they took us out of our comfortable beliefs and ideologies. They have stripped our clothing of certitude and expectations, and saved us from taking things for granted. That is when we surrender to the exploration of the unexpected and bring out of ourselves what we had hidden and didn't know we had.

Practices such as constant isolation, penitential life, and fasting; frequent vigils, praying in uncomfortable ways, kneeling, lotus position, mortifying oneself, or sleeping on hard surfaces satisfy only the ego. It is very much like the Eastern master who one day was polishing a brick. When his disciples asked him what he was doing, he replied, "I'm polishing the brick until it turns into a precious stone." When his disciples replied that that was impossible, he answered, "No more can you become the Buddha through sitting."

The problem with allegorical stories is that we retell them as if they were factual.

We all share in the royal blood: for it is not made of plasma or of illustrious ancestors, but of living spirit. It calls us to awaken the Holy Sparks dormant within hardened shells made up of concepts to enter into our living heritage as children of the Light.

You are heir to a fortune in billions—in fact it already belongs to you, but you somehow got separated early from your family and your family's attorneys can't find you. You ended up living in the streets and killing and stealing in order to eat and are now dumpster diving for your basic sustenance, not knowing that you are wealthy beyond measure. One day someone recognizes you and puts you in touch with the trustees of your fortune. Then you realize that you were never in penury. However, no matter how wealthy you are, if you don't know it, you have no access to it. Not because anyone is denying you, but because you are unaware of your wealth and believe yourself to be poor, alone, and abandoned, when you have never been so.

We are myth makers, poets, and dreamers. Packets of information interacting with each other, we took the appearance of solidity and physicality that we continue to project onto a screen of perception. Transpersonal dreams became, through observation, our conceptual and physical reality. This does not belong to the individual mind alone, but to our collective minds and dreams. We came from the Light as Light and have projected into the world an image. We are artists that have created a painting of a cosmos and have become trapped inside the images—and nightmares—that our dreams have made.

Clothed in physicality we arrive to this planet as secret agents, as emissaries of the Ineffable, entrusted with the mission of reconnecting and healing the fragmented limbs of Divinity that have been broken and scattered within time and space during the process of creation. Several decades are given to each generation to complete its mission. Once our tour of duty ends, the debriefing begins. Did we get lost in the identities we took to complete our mission? Most agents have gone so deep undercover that they have entered the bloodstream of the world and forgotten who they are, their true name, or why they are here; they have put on the values of this world as if they were theirs. May you awaken in your lifetime to the gnosis of who you are and why you took physicality that you may consciously complete the mission given to you. Sleepers, awake! It is your time.

Observing the cosmic drama unfolding before us in which we are all involved, often as unwilling participants. Few are those who are conscious of its origins or of why and what's actually happening. Fewer yet understand its destiny and purpose.

Everything tells the story. I doubt that most people really know why they say most things. I feel that there is a force in us wanting to be heard and tell its story—a variety of stories, but all pointing to love and freedom. We think that it is one subject, but it is transpersonal and goes beyond the individual telling, so we resonate with the story, but often fail to hear the message or identify the Sender.

Woe to the person who lets their experience consume them, and blessed is the person who walks through this world awakened and alive to every moment, free from the straightjacket of their handed-down beliefs.

No genuine external transformation occurs unless it has first happened internally. Of course, the world does not know the difference. A person must have eyes to see and ears to hear. "The light shines on in the dark and the darkness understands it not. Many people say that they want to wake up. They speak accurately when they perceive their lives as nightmarish. Not so if the wake-up call arrives when they like the dream they are having. Have you ever met anyone who thanks you for attempting to wake them up, even if they asked you to do so the night before, while they are in the midst of enjoying a pleasant dream? Much that goes for spirituality is just so much fluff—pleasant dreams that keep the seeker from ever passing through the Gates.

The role of the snake in the garden is to open the eyes of the innocent, blinded tillers of the land. It reveals the Deceiver, the vengeful, tantrum-prone false god that attempted to keep its creation blind to the God above god, the God of mercy and compassion. It is to these exiled children of Eve that the clear task of redeeming humanity and all its Kingdoms, living in this valley of tears, has been given. Avatars of the ineffable God come to us from age to age, as in the example of Christ, Buddha, and others; those who show the way to freedom, that the ruler may not prevail. All this is done with mercy and compassion. Awakening is the revelation that opens the eyes to the conditioning that has been passed from generation to generation. May all beings awaken, may all sentient beings be free.

Believe none of the above. Read with eyes free of the millennia of conditioning that perpetuates the blindness to what has been taught.

Humanity has received a mission other than doing, producing, accumulating goods, reproducing, information, and power. Humanity has received the mission of being ever more intimate with the One who is Being itself, who is Love and Trust itself, to the point of union. Repose. Be at rest. Allow the awareness of being filled with divine grace to descend, rest upon, unite, and awaken that which is within you.

It is as if we are all sunk in quicksand; we are no less human for having fallen into the quagmire, yet we cannot extricate ourselves or the others who are caught in it with us without the light-power's help; we require someone outside of the quicksand to lift us out. Also, in our predicament of ignorance and forgetfulness, we require one who knows us from our divine origin to remind us of who we are.

The essential pointing to our true nature is simple and possible for everyone, including children, to grasp. However, it can take some time to empty and free our minds from the concepts we cherish about who we consider ourselves to be.

GNOSIS...

I cannot say that I first came to conscious awareness of gnosis through a glimpse of light in the darkness. Rather, it happened through the loss of light and descent into darkness.

Originally, gnosis was there, as close as my own heartbeat and as naturally a part of me as breathing. I was not, however, conscious of it because I had never been apart from it. My awareness was of an extraordinary Presence that sometimes was much stronger than at other times. And then, suddenly, it was gone.

I was nineteen years old when I first experienced in my own flesh the cruelty of the world. Living with my family in Castro's Cuba, I was taken a political prisoner at a secret police headquarters, where I was repeatedly beaten and brutally tortured. I was raped by I don't know how many soldiers. It seemed like one hundred but may have been only twelve or fifteen. That was when I lost it! That was when I lost that sense of the Presence. That loss was worse than all the torture, rape, and other cruelties. It was an experience of something that was like a reverse cosmic consciousness. A sense of aloneness. The absence of that Presence. There was no joy, no hope, no life. Some days later I was returned to my cell after more beatings and torture. It was then, sitting alone in agony, that I had a staggering experience. I overheard *a conversation between two of the soldiers. One of them was the officer in charge. He had never smiled. Some of the others would smile sarcastically or tauntingly and chide me, but this one never did. He never touched me, but he was the one who would give the orders to the others of what was to be done. He frightened me the most. He was the most terrifying individual I had ever encountered. He embodied all the dark images of the Catholic Satan. He was a monster. For the first time in my life I saw something that seemed totally evil. Until then I had never believed in total evil. One day I heard this monster speaking very enthusiastically-the first time he had ever been so animated. I looked out of my cell at him, and he had the brightest smile on his face. That made me very curious. This monster can smile? He can speak with enthusiasm? He was talking about how he had gotten a puppy for his daughter and how excited he was to be giving it to her. He was full of love and enthusiasm in anticipating his little girl's joy at seeing that puppy. I thought, can he have a little girl? Does he love a little girl?*

Then I saw that light aspect of him, his capability of loving his child just like any human parent. of loving a dog just as I would love my dog. That was a horrifying experience for me. For it meant that the man was not so utterly different from me, that he could love like me, that even he had some light inside him. Even worse, it meant that his darkness, his horror, must also exist potentially in me. So while we had different inclinations, we were still made of the same cloth. All of my life until then I had devoted to God. Having considered spending my life in a convent, I had offered myself as a bargaining tool to God for the sake of humanity, offering myself as a sacrifice to compensate for the pain of the world. The realization that came to me in a Cuban jail annihilated this one-sided view of my tormentor. Humanity no longer existed as a set of opposites but was more like a fabric interwoven of light and dark threads. I could no longer leave the darkness behind. Once I accepted the wholeness of life, once I accepted darkness as an integral part of humanity, my prayer for all of life without rejection exploded within me. Hopelessness ended, and I was totally possessed by joy. The Presence once again filled my being. Pain was still there, but suffering was not. This time I did not take the experience of the Presence to be as common and natural as breathing. I now recognized it as wholly Other. It infused every atom of my humanity, yet it remained distinct from me.

My words come from firsthand experience and observation, and are not derived secondhand from the thoughts of others. I often quote Gnostic, Buddhist, Christian, Sufi, Jewish, Hindu and other material when they aptly illustrate what I'm saying. I'm not interpreting the original statements, just applying them to mine. I'm not a follower of Gnostic, Christian or any other teachings, but of God that dwells in me and in all living things

---

A word on how I use the word gnosis. Once the experience of gnosis is processed by the thought, it is no longer gnosis, so it becomes just words that may sound good and be even helpful, wise and inspiring. I'm not saying that that person has not had a powerful experience and may have even reached a milestone in their path, but not all experiences are of gnosis. I use the word experience when speaking of gnosis, but it is not an experience because at that level of perception there is *no experiencer.* Once the experiencer, or "I," comes into play, it has already become the product of thought and human interpretation, which is always filtered through previous experiences and conditioning.

Any teaching, practice or tradition designed to connect us to the Source cannot be based on belief. It can't be about concepts. It can only be about observing, testing, and knowing in the actual, immediate, direct experience of this moment. We can always change what we believe if presented with better arguments, logic, and evidence, but we can't unknow what we know when we have experienced it firsthand.

Gnosis depends on our knowing that whatever we know is infinitesimally smaller than what we don't know. Gnostics know that we don't know. Gnosis is present in the moment. Gnostics are not believers. Believing means that we have accepted a number of things that we have read or have been told that we don't know. Even our own experiences, if we interpret them according to our beliefs, become part of our ignorance, for they have died and missed the chance of being gnosis.

In Greek *gnosis*refers to a special type of knowledge, a mystical firsthand enlightenment. The mistake that many people make in using the word is that they do not differentiate gnosis from other types of knowledge defined by different Greek words that are not gnosis. Gnosis is differentiated from other types of knowledge, such as *doxa*, or belief, opinion, dogma, or the "right" belief; *episteme*, such as scientific knowledge or as in Plato's definition of "justified true belief"; *techne*, which is more commonly translated as art, craft, and craftsmanship. For instance, magic would be more aptly termed *techne* instead of *gnosis*; meditation techniques are *techne*, although they may lead to *gnosis*. The various religious beliefs would go under *doxa*, and the scientifically explored part of spirituality and study of belief would be more appropriately called *episteme*.

Gnosis does not depend on belief, but remains the untranslatable experience of something that for lack of any appropriate word we call God, and that while known intimately, still remains alien and unknowable in concepts and words. Words, poetry, mythology, symbol, dance, music, and ritual can be used as if they were fingers pointing to the moon, but they are not the moon. Existing mythologies of any tradition, including Gnostic myths, can serve as signposts, but none are gnosis itself, because all are efforts of the mind to express the inexpressible. Gnostic and other myths present a story told from diverse angles attempting to explain our origins, our saga, and our completion. While none are factual, they are all true and powerful depending on how one unpacks the symbols that may reveal something entirely different than what they seem to say at first hearing.

Gnosis comes spontaneously and from it poetry and stories may develop; however, if dogmas develop, gnosis cannot remain fresh and alive, outside of time, revealing and liberating. When dogmas arise, gnosis does not. The luminous experience is replaced by a new caricature pretending to be something that it can never reach.

We cannot effectively process newly acquired knowledge with the same mindset that held the old worldview. This is essentially so when speaking of gnosis. Gnosis itself brings about a new, fundamentally transformed mindset, the result of an internal revolution at the very roots of thought, except when this mutation is aborted by holding on to the old thought processing system. Without this radical transformation, what was a powerful illumination turns shortly after into just another new belief, with only an increasingly dim memory remaining of one big, shining moment.

Any attempt to understand gnosis (mystical experience) through concepts is doomed to miss the point because of the unspeakable nature of the experience. As in the past, gnosis continues to challenge the certitudes of the times.

Every existing thing turns to dust. Every belief may be replaced with a better formulated concept. New scholarly and scientific discoveries make all knowledge obsolete. Another type of knowing exists. This we call gnosis, although it may not resemble everything called Gnosticism. This knowing exists beyond all beginnings. It originates outside time. Different cultures may call it by different names, but the names are not this gnosis. All touched by this experience understand each other. It is the same for all because it bypasses ego, conditioning, and personality. It can never be "my gnosis" or "your gnosis." Only gnosis.

Inbreaks of the Divine require a flexible mind capable of letting go of every acquired concept of God. Gnosis is quite different from religious, historical, and any other kind of knowledge. One emerges from within, throwing open our inner gates; the other comes from without.

Gnosis has to do with spiritual and cosmic knowledge that is not received through empirical means. Something akin to *moksha*, very similar to Buddha's liberation, but with sharp teeth. Don't ask me what I mean by the teeth. Those who know will understand.

I bring you hints and pieces of the cosmic puzzle and deliberately place them in everything I write. They do not fit into old containers, and interpretations in familiar, accepted ways will fail. Anamnesis may rise like incense smoke, not through the intellect, but through their scent, taste, and flavor. If allowed to linger in your palate and permitted to enter the skin and work themselves into the larger pattern to which they belong without accepting or rejecting them, they shall reveal their secrets—not to your thoughts, but to your soul. Then the arrows must be caught in flight, for high speed flying arrows they are, and they won't be caught by the conditioned mind.

The explicit purpose for which I write consists in exercising, stretching, and activating the rarely used and unfamiliar section of the brain through which we perceive gnosis. This is not the same part of the brain that perceives and processes physical and conceptual realities. I don't give the scientific names of those sections of the brain on purpose in order to avoid the human habit of believing that knowing the name of something means knowing and understanding that something. That's why discussions, arguments for or against anything, historicity, academic Gnosticism, current varied scientific paradigms and religious structures of any kind fall outside the parameters of my teaching. I'm not minimizing their value within the familiar brain, and there are many places where they may be discussed—but not here.

Gnosis very often appears in poetry, scripture, and many other writings by authors who have not only *not* read the Nag Hammadi Library or other gnostic texts, but have never even heard the word gnosis. Gnosis does not come from the so-called gnostic writings, but it came before Gnosticism and before anything pertaining to it was ever put into words. Gnosis still comes in that manner to this day.

Gnosis is not rational or logical in the Greek sense, it cannot be proven empirically. Only people tuned to the same channel, who can tune to the same level, are able to understand what a mystic conveys in word symbols. That's why the churches and institutions cannot understand Yeshua's teachings; that's why most scholars and people in general cannot understand Gnostic texts. This understanding occurs in a realm beyond the mental ego. Gnosis is not knowledge or education as the world understands these words; knowledge and education are not the same as transformation. Only those tuned to the same channel can understand the teachings of a mystic.

Gnosis remains a secret to all except the pneumatic. Not because its secrets are hidden, but because of the nature of the hearer. The hylic and the psychic hear the same words as the pneumatic, and although they think they understand, they do so only at their level, but have no idea of the fullness of their meaning. It's a secret so deceptively simple, so often sung and written of in poetry—even shouted from the rooftops—that it's mostly missed. When this secret has been directly revealed, it has been dismissed as unimportant. And so, a whole system of austerities, initiations, and elite hierarchies have been created around it because the human mind so often refuses to see what's blatantly standing in front of it. Any teaching or practice or tradition designed to connect us to the source cannot be based on belief. It can't be about concepts. It can only be about observing, testing, and knowing the actual, immediate, direct experience of this moment.

Whatever one may say that gnosis is, it is not. If we can fill in the blank "gnosis is —," that is, explaining it in cataphatic terms, know that that's not what I mean by gnosis, but it is just an interpretation of it. We can only say what is not (apophasis), for words come from thought and gnosis precedes thought. You, who read these words, either know of what I speak or do not. What you know you cannot *un*know. Everything else is speculation and guesswork. Gnosis is only a word unless you experience it firsthand. Until then, it is just hearsay. Gnosis appears as a result of a consciousness-altering flash. It appears in full eternal bloom from the uncreated Source from which it springs. It does not translate into words, although the brain spends a lifetime doing its best to express it.

What is known is all around us. It is scattered like seeds everywhere. But seeds don't germinate unless they fall on fertile ground. The mind that is ready for gnosis catches the hints like catching an arrow in flight. If the mind is cluttered with conditioning and tends to think in any particular direction, be it "spiritual" or worldly, it will not help that mind, at least not immediately, no matter how clearly the teaching is given. There's a kinship of the spirit among those touched by Source while still living in flesh. That touch is consciously known and independent of any form of belief.

There are people who have assumed that I do not consider gnosis to be intuitive. It is not that I don't consider gnosis intuitive, it is just that gnosis is not even an "it." I'm not minimizing the value of intuition or even the words of others. I'm only saying that gnosis, or direct unmediated knowing, a knowing that has nothing to do with knowledge as we use the word in English, belongs to another order that bypasses everything known, even intuition. I'm not being evasive in my answers. It is just that the only way to speak of "it" is in apophatic terms or of what is not. Each person who has been seized by the Mystery describes it in his or her own word symbols and according to the audience they are trying to reach, although they know that only those who have been there can understand it. Like at the event at Pentecost, the spiritual polyglot needs no translation. The mind must be fresh for gnosis. It may visit briefly in a moment of clarity, but it doesn't make its home in a space cluttered by assumptions, beliefs and the words of others, no matter how wise. It is never secondhand.

One major impediment to communication involving gnosis and any type of direct experience derives from the prevalent beliefs and language that most people calling themselves spiritual share. New information and possibilities become automatically translated through what they already believe in. Those beliefs are fiercely protected from harm. In the rare chance of a realization that something different is being heard, the hearer (armored with an already existing lingo and worldview) instinctively, unconsciously, and immediately manages to reduce the new into the old, reducing both the messenger and the news into something manageable that bears no resemblance to the teaching imparted. Unless the arrow is caught in flight, waking the sleeper in the middle of the dream, a new dream is created but there is no arrow and the hand is empty.

I don't interpret texts. Instead I depart from the opposite direction. What I directly experience and live comes first, then sometimes, when I'm writing, a saying or a whole text suddenly springs up glowing brightly in my mind's eye, as if infused with golden, molten light. Those I use, as they illustrate my writing. I don't write or teach anything from the outside in, but from firsthand experience out.

Once gnosis invades an individual, every cell becomes suffused with gnosis. All beliefs, platitudes, unquestioned values, fears, and memes with which people are conditioned since birth are completely destroyed. All intellectual constructs fall apart. Not only the personal world changes, but it is the whole world that changes, within and without. Gnosis utterly transforms the individual's perception of reality. As with gnosis, even if weak and poor, your own unwrapping of your firsthand experience is better than the most complex secondhand treatise on religion.

We encounter gnosis through a different part of the brain than the familiar one that we use to perceive and process physical and conceptual realities. Certain types of people become awake in these different regions that do not receive their input from outer reality. That input cannot be translated into concrete, ordinary words or even enter into the realm of thought. However, our familiar brain processes want to capture, cage, study, and understand the unfamiliar, but by its very nature it cannot succeed. Gnosis always remains unfamiliar to that thinking part of the brain.

There are many types of knowledge and all are useful and some even necessary in this world, but what I mean by gnosis belongs to another order. It belongs to the experience of the direct, first-hand touch by the Eternal. Even the word experience is inappropriate for what I'm attempting to describe and only those who have at least felt that touch can truly understand.

The familiar brain with its own created identity can never know, although it would love to do it and call itself pneumatic, which it is not. Only the awakened, unfamiliar part of the brain knows that it knows, but it also knows that what it knows cannot be translated into the familiar.

The gnosis of which I speak has nothing to do with religions, the intellect, feelings, or even intuition. It is not any kind of "ism," including Gnosticism or any kind of intimate familiarity with the works of others. It is never derivative or secondhand.

It is a different type of knowing. No amount of imagination, belief, or scholarly knowledge can prepare one for the devastating experience of That. The word God doesn't even begin to cover that Encounter that annihilates every concept, belief, or "knowledge." The rest is just chasing bright shadows, confusing images with Presence. Just as in the myth of Sophia, we take our projections for Reality, mate with them, and give birth to defective offspring that we name religions.

Our brain comes fully endowed with the potential to experience the inbreak of God into human consciousness. Depending on the depth, power, and duration of this inbreak, we may experience it as gnosis, anointment, and grace. Attempts to diminish it or explain it away with various scientific, religious, and other jargon doesn't change what happens. What happens restructures us from the inside out, affecting our brain and worldview in multiple ways, no matter what sophisticated sophistries we may use to explain the unexplainable away. This is why bidden or unbidden, God won't go away.

Belief systems tend to wed the believer to images and concepts, conditioning the believer to look for support for what they already believe or to find theories to fit the concepts they have held thus far. While seekers may adopt beliefs based on Gnosticism, beliefs are not gnosis. Beliefs have no part in the experience of gnosis. Gnosis cannot be described or spoken of except in apophatic terms; that is to say, in terms of what is not. It has no resemblance to anything conceived by the mind. Nakedness of the mind, a full stop to thought, precedes the moment of illumination or gnosis. As long as the mind clings to its old assumed wisdom, mystical experiences remain temporary epiphanies rather than gnosis.

Gnosis reveals itself to the one who knows nothing. This holy ignorance does not derive from lack of knowledge, but from a dazzling type of knowing that eclipses all we previously thought was knowledge.

Blessed are those who know that they don't know, for the doors to gnosis may open its possibilities to them.

Breakthroughs, epiphanies, and flashes of understanding come to us like blessed drops on parched lips during our earth journey. At those moments, everything seems to finally make sense. Wonderful and useful as these breakthroughs are, they are not gnosis. Concepts and beliefs, even those based on Gnostic texts are not gnosis. No definition exists and no container can hold gnosis, no matter how much we yearn to bring some words that would link gnosis to human understanding; and yet, we know with a knowing that the brain cannot hold. Only apophatic language that tells us what is not is possible. If it can enter the human mind, it is not gnosis.

The experience of gnosis—or mystical experience, as I prefer to call it, as that name is more universal and cannot be confused with any sectarian connotations—tells us that the true reality is always here in this moment. There is only this timeless dance that life carries out in evolution. The meaning of the dance is not found in its coming to an end. It is found in the dance itself.

Gnosis or mysticism doesn't necessarily have to express itself in a sweetly pious vocabulary, as if mystic states had something to do with church-mouse religiosity. Rather, mysticism is the experience of the everyday, of the here and now. This experience can be altogether banal. It can be had on a dunghill as well as in a fragrant garden, in the blowing wind or in a religious ceremony.

In the first second that you look at something for the first time there is a silence and a quietness, and then the mind says, "what's the name of that?" If that solitary, initial moment before asking is stretched and maintained before naming, then perhaps there may be gnosis.

Whatsoever enters the mind—taste, touch, sound—be there. Be conscious of the first moment when there is no labeling, no defining, no comparing, no liking nor disliking, and if you become conscious of it you'll find the moments outside of time becoming longer and without the need to automatically label anything or move to the next thing or wanting something new, for everything is new and fresh each time. There is a movement that is not vertical and is not horizontal and that moves without space and without time and that never changes and is never the same.

The path to Gnosis is the path of the heart, not a path of the head as some understand knowledge. This path is not difficult when you have no preferences, when you can allow whatever happens to be okay. Grace emerges when you permit yourself to be borne along in and by the Way, when you feel no need to control the situation. It is an unspeakable grace to simply be, with no need to do. This is so because it is humankind's natural state, our original state. It is the state in which we are consciously in and one with the Mind of God.

Divine sources, whose gnosis cannot be transmitted by words alone, tend to be forgotten and replaced by fables, dreams, and myths. These may still work as long as we remember that these are only pointers toward other Realities, but are not the Realities themselves.

GNOSTIC...

I'm often asked what kind of Gnostic I am, whether Valentinian, Sethian, Phildickian, etc. Why limit myself so? I don't follow any of them. I transmit what comes directly from Source, not as a choice, but as a prior act of surrender to the Ineffable Being that acts of its own volition. In this, no limitation exists, but an open, infinite wealth to which we are heir if we dare to humbly accept our inheritance.

I am a Teacher, a Bishop, and a Hierophant in both my traditions of Esoteric/Mystical/Gnostic Ecclesia and of the Holy Order of Miriam of Magdala. I have experienced oneness and know myself to be beyond any path. But I cannot initiate someone or bless someone into Buddhism, although I can do it in the Vedanta path of Hinduism because I have received initiation into it. Nor can an Eastern Master do so with someone following my path. But all Teachers of all paths can (and do) recognize and rejoice in each other, knowing that they are in the presence of another who has transcended paths and has become the Way.

The gnostic mystic is aware of the impermanence of things and does not expect more of them than they can give. Freedom does not depend on outer things, but is an immutable state beyond the things of this world.

We don't decide to become Gnostics, but we discover that's what we were all along. We don't adhere to beliefs or views imposed from the outside, but our worldview comes from our inner experience. Sometimes that experience comes with the sound of cannons. Most of the time it happens quietly and gently but is nevertheless life altering, even though an external observer won't notice the difference. We are un-made and remade from the inside out, never from the outside in. To be a gnostic, one must first be an agnostic.

To be a passerby we need to drop our personal agendas, even our religious ones. From such a mind comes generosity without thinking that we are giving; courage, without thinking that we are brave; full acceptance and embracing, without thinking we are tolerant; wisdom, without needing to change anyone else; transformation, without thinking that we are changing.

For the awakened, once an unpleasant event is over, it is finished. If remembered, it is only a memory without substance. The same with physical pain once it is over. They happen only as long as they are happening and no longer, leaving no emotional content. The psyche does not perpetuate their moment. Their value, if any, is extracted immediately, as it is happening, while the husk is automatically discarded. Others seem to enjoy living in the past, reliving each received insult, loss, ego injury, nurturing them as if they were valued treasure. They carry them as badges of honor, nurturing resentment, and suffering tremendously, until they tire of the drama and its power dissipates. Then they'll begin living again, breathing freely, the burden lifted. I noticed this since early childhood at my mother's house, producing its rejection and spontaneous initiation into the first type. When an event is over, it is ended, without leftover residue, for it exists no more.

The ancient dictum that the adept can only communicate with the adept works at many levels. Language takes a different meaning when the key has been turned and the world of pneuma has flung its doors wide open. The pneumatic then functions fully not only in pneuma, but in the worlds psyche and hyle, without abandoning them, even though he or she simultaneously moves through a different world. It is more than intuition. He or she thinks differently and in an unimaginable fashion. The very functioning of the brain has been altered. Secrets are secret not because they are concealed, but because the ordinary function of the brain, even in highly intelligent and very spiritual individuals cannot apprehend them until pneuma has opened to them. The pneumatic functions in all worlds without duality, but only other pneumatics can fully communicate with them. It is a solitary world, even when surrounded by friends, although there is never loneliness.

Not all that claim the name "Gnostic" have been touched and transformed by gnosis. Not all genuine gnostics have ever heard of the name.

Gnostics are as varied as the different sects of Christianity; some of them even more so. The one thing they have in common with one another is that the Divine Mystery is experiential and not an article of belief. Early Gnostics ranged from the ascetic to the libertine. Some could be dogmatic and some, like this one, were freethinkers and not bound by any specific cultural tradition or religious belief.

The yearning of the Gnostic in this world gives voice to something deeper struggling to emerge. Its roots often remain unrecognized or intentionally ignored.

The Gnostic does not see the world in opposition. S/he can hold more than two seemingly contradictory views simultaneously and without conflict. Indeed, it is difficult for a person trying to impose that functioning by an act of the will because s/he finds this attitude desirable. The attitude I describe derives naturally and without will or effort from the inner, pneumatic state and is not something that a person decides to do.

The Gnostic is neither an ascetic nor a theologian and need not even be particularly religious in the conventional way. The Gnostic is an artist. The Gnostic's brushes, colors, and canvasses are her own body, his own psyche. The Gnostic's technique is one of living and observing life and recognizing it for what it is, without illusions of security, glamor, or despair. The Gnostic continually explores, always seeking the core of the nature of things. But gnosis, like art, cannot be taught. The flame of living gnosis awakens and rises of its own accord. All we can provide is a nest within our heart, a sanctuary of repose where the breath of the Divine may whisper its secrets.

The mystic (gnostic), as I use the term, receives instruction from the source and does not follow second hand statements. Some of those statements shine from the brilliance of gnosis because they come from gnosis, and the mystic uses those passages of scriptures to *illustrate*, not to interpret, teachings that cannot be spoken of directly, and never as something to follow or believe in. I must add a caveat. By mystic and gnosis, I don't mean strong feelings and assumptions that people classify as "knowing;" I don't mean New Age beliefs and I don't share a lingua franca with New Age terms, concepts and interpretations; it does not mean psychic visions, although they are not always excluded. Whatever assumptions can be made of any of my statements are just that, assumptions. There I am speaking apophatically again!

We return to everyday reality carrying no memory of a moment that cannot be called a moment, for it is beyond time. Untouched by thought or memory, but with senses atingle with knowledge beyond knowledge that always remains unknown, every living cell remains a witness to the extraordinary, even as they replicate themselves. We are forever branded with its flavor, haunted by its longing, peace, and forbidden knowledge, bearing Emptiness's unbearable secret.

Some fear the darkness and the void, but it is in the vastness of emptiness that fullness dwells, and where darkness is nothing but unutterable radiance.

What strikes the casual reader of the Gnostic texts at first glance is the abundance of feminine and sexual imagery in descriptions of divinity, Christ, and myths of creation and cosmology.

Gnostics existed before Gnostic systems and even the name Gnostic came into being. The phenomenon has always been. Gnostic writings and mythologies derive from gnosis; gnosis does not derive from Gnostic mythologies. Gnosis does not appear from their study, although they may help by pointing to it and even by acting as catalysts. We do not acquire or convert to a belief, but discover that we have been Gnostics all along once we find there is a name for it. Gnosis spontaneously emerges from within and without us simultaneously, putting everything together like pieces of a jigsaw puzzle. Like dancing, it moves and flows through us, effortlessly installing itself in us, but for most people there can be stages of gnosis. At the earliest stages, many begin expounding on everything, believing themselves full Gnostics because of the initial illumination; however, one of the key characteristics of a gnostic consists in clearly knowing what they don't know. Like Christianity and any other system of metaphors, Gnosticism all too often becomes an ideology rather than a means to liberation.

At the Gates, they meet "The Guardians of the Threshold," to use a mystery tradition term. The Guardians appear as terrifying, filling the traveler with sinking fear, for the images arise from the cauldron of their internal forces. They think that the Chief Guardian is God. Many who go through the Gates never go beyond them, thinking that they have arrived at the plenitude of knowledge, not knowing that it is only the Threshold. Instead of negotiating passage, they just want to escape. Early Gnostics called that state "The Midst." While the ones that arrived there have gone far, and no longer get fooled by the dream, they remain in a nowhere land. They need to know that their stop is just temporary and eventually, they may move further, but not while they are convinced that theirs is the meaning of Gnosis. I call those ones "pessimistic Gnostics."

Since my late teenage years, I saw that the suffering, violence and cruelty of this world could not be attributed to only human failing or that some form of disobedience (sin) caused this condition. It seemed that this flaw, this rift, was inherent in the fabric of the world. This put me completely in the camp of the ancient heresy of the Gnostics. Seeing God as whole and complete without duality while simultaneously contemplating the duality and fragmentation of the world, I sensed that there's also something else, like a parasite, that stands between us and God. Three of the manifestations of that parasite come in the forms of control, authoritarianism, and psychological time.

Writers of Gnostic sacred scriptures, as well as mystic treatises, poetry etc., clothe in words and concepts their experience and interpretation of the experience. In those writings the signature of the Beloved may suddenly appear in a flash of insight in 3D, even when hidden in images and works of fiction. We must remember, however, that insight does not come through another person's interpretation, no matter how brilliant and inspired the writer may be. Gnosis can only be received directly from the Source that infuses and illumines our minds and bestows sight to ordinary eyes.

Many schools of Gnosticism flourished in the first few centuries of the first Millennium, although gnosis preceded the arrival of Gnosticism and Christianity. Like now, the one thing all those diverse and even conflicting schools had in common is that all sentient beings come impregnated with a Spark of the Divine. It is through self knowledge and not through intellectual knowledge—or knowledge gained through analysis—that we discover our eternal being. That eternal spark is one with Being and has nothing to do with the God created by the projections of human thought.

The gnostic does not try to escape suffering, but experiences it deeply, not blaming God or others, but knowing his or her role in this world. This gnostic not only realizes that there is suffering, but enters deeply into hell while simultaneously living within a different internal state, one in which peace and joy remain immovable. He or she does not postpone gnosis, wisdom, and bliss until the lion is laying down with the lamb but knows that gnosis is paramount to fully functioning in the hell that this world often presents to us in order to fulfill his or her human and divine destiny. This gnostic is an Urban Mystic, a secret agent, an antibody in the bloodstream of the world. May the eternal mystery be completed through us.

URBAN MYSTIC...

The Beloved instructed me through every eye that looked at me. Not all of those eyes were human eyes ... I was guided to gnosis again and again, solely by the silent prompting of that wholly Other resounding in my heart. .... As the vision unfolded, the lens of my mind opened wider to encompass a numinous Presence that is totally beyond even words such as "love" and "God." I crossed an abyss by the end of which all human logic and knowledge crumbled. All theologies, philosophies, and beliefs dissolved, as if they had never been. Finally, I dissolved into the Presence. And then the lens slowly narrowed. It narrowed enough to permit me to move within that Presence yet still be capable of functioning on a day-to-day basis. None of these words must ever be confused with the experience itself. The Lovers of the Beloved can meet anywhere, be it a park, a house, a café, or a restaurant. External sounds become background music coming as if from a distant dimension. Any place can be our temple, where the aliveness of the moment transforms all things.

Since as early as I can remember, since before I could speak, I have been carried in the flow of a Love and all-encompassing sense of Presence that I shall call Mystery because no name can contain it. It is first-hand experience, and I find resonance in the poetry of mystics and in the words of some of the early and modern Gnostics. That was only the beginning of a never-ending mystical journey.

It takes a certain knack to live in ecstasy and communion while paying taxes, hearing police and ambulance sirens, neighbors arguing with each other, garbage trucks, and smelling bus exhaust and city fumes from below. That knack is the mark of the Urban Mystic.

Early on I was aware that God existed beyond time; no yesterday, today, or tomorrow—just now, everything is now. I'm using the word now, but I was unconvinced that God was the proper name for what I experienced. I just wondered if that *something* people called God was the same *something* I knew. The more I read in some quarters about God, the less it sounded like what I knew, until I came in contact with the poetry of mystics and, when they used "God" and better yet, "Beloved," I recognized what I was trying to name.

Mysticism is a word we use for the full immersion in divine love. It is an experience widely reported by followers not only of Jesus but of other religions. This experience of oneness with

God, however we describe it, binds us together across boundaries of creed and tradition.

The Urban Mystic has a foot in each world, the ineffable and the mundane, having the ability of dancing between them with grace and assurance. The Urban Mystic lives consciously and simultaneously in more than one world, as they interpenetrate each other.

Urban Mystic is a term that, as wild gnosis, I have coined because I could not find one that existed that meant what I mean. The Urban Mystic speaks with a voice that does not need the approval, agreement, recognition or respectability of the world.

I also use the metaphor of the surfer, when life seems to overwhelm us, like a wave too big to handle. The experienced surfer becomes exhilarated by the danger. At that moment there is no thought of past victories or failures, or dreams of future ones; of no job or personal life. Only our riding the wave remains present, as it builds and finally crashes. Attention does not waver. That's the type of attention needed in meditation and mindfulness, that's living in eternity; not just for a moment, an hour, or a day—but fully awake every moment of our lives.

In my experience I have found that there is more in common among the mystics of different traditions than there is with many followers of their own traditions. Thus, my favorite quote from Louis-Claude de Saint-Martin, "All mystics speak the same language for they come from the same country."

Governments and empires rise and fall, religions come and go, ideologies and political philosophies wax and wane, but the experience of the mystics remains a fixed star in the human firmament. Even when dogmatic establishments try to eradicate them, they keep popping back up. They come wild, without claiming any existing system, or they come within recognized traditions. They are known by many names, but in their essential nature they act as secret agents for the awesome Mystery.

The Urban Mystic accepts the world as it is—the ugliness alongside the beauty, and toughness tempered with gentleness, humor, and humility. This mystic remains conscious that suffering is the neighbor of joy. This individual lives poised between two worlds, aware of the reality beyond opposites. Sometimes it is like walking on a tightrope in the darkness across an abyss guided only by the light within the heart, a light brighter than the noonday sun.

The Urban mystic recognizes the moments when archetypal realities and worldly events coincide in either the history of the world or in our personal histories. The Timeless intersects time, and in those instances we can feel that the gods are walking the earth—sometimes in a malevolent manner and others in supremely benevolent ways—all part of a dance of cosmic proportions. At these inbreaks of God, whether in our lives or in the world, infinite possibilities arise and the impossible becomes possible, depending on our personal and collective awareness and skill. May grace and compassion always be our guides at every step we take, especially when the veils become thin and the exchange opens.

The mystic is never young and never ages although the earthly body bears the mark of years. In time, like all matter, it releases its essence and resolves to its origins. Aging needs time and the mystic's world knows not of time.

The language of the mystic is a non-language hidden behind their words. Spoken and written language serve as symbols that point elsewhere, for words lend themselves to different interpretations that breed misunderstandings and even injury. Mystics speak the language of their shared country; a sub-language in which communication is constantly happening at a deeper level. It doesn't matter in what tradition the mystic speaks or what words they use. They come from the same country and thus understand each other's tongue. I have often compared their words to capsules carrying the antibody within them. Capsules come in different colors, sizes, and shapes, but the salvific medicine they contain remains the same. Of course, I mean something very specific when I say the word "mystic." We don't all mean exactly the same thing when using that word.

The poet asks the Soul: Are there words that can communicate what is beyond thought and feeling? Are there words that would not impede immediate perception or invite polemic, but words that would throw open gates of worlds within worlds in a single instant?

The mystic's experience of the indescribable and ineffable finds expression in the language of myth, ritual, poetry, and theater. Myth happens out of time. The story takes on a life of its own and becomes the re-enactment of a cosmic mystery play. The stories contain their own meaning, never to be confused with historical events. To understand them we need to shift beyond religious beliefs, academic understanding of the words, and the need to prove a particular point. Story and art resonate with something formless, revealing beyond them an encounter with the transforming power of the moment, a mystical insight that at its most profound level we call gnosis.

Urban Mystics convey metaphors for which no concepts are possible in language that seems more like enrapturing erotica or brazen heresy than approved theology. Many had to write commentaries in order to survive. As a young mystic, I often made efforts to communicate. However, each can only understand depending on the perspective seen from where they are standing. That's why I don't bother translating, as each must catch the arrow in flight.

We find duality and multiplicity in the world of form as we perceive it according to our concepts. Or we may subscribe to the view of unity and Oneness, especially after having had a mystical experience. But both views by themselves miss the mark in their incompleteness. Another dimension presents itself in a third vista that experiences both worlds at once and without conflict. This third view reveals not only the slower frequencies of the world of gross objects and memories but it simultaneously presents the awareness of living in a world of oneness and quantum reality as well as what exists in between.

The spiritual polyglot does not need everything spelt out for them. Mystics are such linguists. We can use either male or female terms and any word for God handy at the moment and still understand the message. Each person that has been seized by the Mystery describes it in his or her own word symbols and according to the audience they are trying to reach, although they know that only those who have been there can understand it. Like at the event at Pentecost, the spiritual polyglot needs no translation.

The mystic does not beg God, as if God were an overlord whose favor we need to propitiate. We approach God as a lover; as lovers who have no secrets from each other and no shame. We give ourselves to the Supreme Mystery not groveling, but wantonly.

To be a passerby we need to drop our personal agendas, even our religious ones. From such a mind comes generosity without thinking that we are giving; courage, without thinking that we are brave; full acceptance and embracing, without thinking we are tolerant; wisdom, without needing to change anyone else; transformation, without thinking that we are changing.

It is easy to act enlightened and filled with gratitude when personal and surrounding circumstances are relatively fine. It is when tragedy strikes and loss, betrayal, persecution, and adversity come along that we recognize the mark of the Urban mystic; for it is at those times that their light shines most brightly. The mystic moves in the eye of the hurricane and meets all situations with the same equanimity.

The Urban Mystic works in secret, acting as an antibody in the bloodstream of humanity and religion. Rather than avoiding the world, this being chooses to function and thrive within it while not being influenced by it. Not caught in duality, this mystic remains aware of multiple dimensions of reality. The Urban Mystic observes suffering alongside beauty and compassion. This being takes discordant city noises with the same peace and equanimity as nature's song while still having preferences. The Urban Mystic, while not necessarily pious or even religious, lives poised between the worlds aware of the Reality beyond opposites, awake and connected to the Source no matter what form the moment takes.

Some days I feel like Leonardo da Vinci when he said, "It vexes me greatly that having to earn my living has forced me to interrupt the work and to attend to small matters." Then I quickly remember that no matter what I'm doing, I'm doing the work for the sake of which I have disguised myself in a body.

Each time a mystic opens a line between the fog of this world and the "ground of Being," the collective stream of consciousness lights up in the darkness. These mystics do not sell out to the counterfeit forces that masquerade as culture and exoteric religions. The conditioned mind with its literal interpretations stand as obstacles to this immense opening. They enslave body and soul with their need for consensus. May your hearing hear beyond the spoken and written words. May your vision pierce the darkness like a laser beam. May you not be swayed by the thoughts of the world. May every breathing being awaken in an all-encompassing lifting of the Divine Sparks that compose all things.

Indeed, there is no separation between the Source and ourselves, except in our awareness. Being a mystic, I'm often in ecstasy at this bountiful presence. Sadly, misery, injustice, and cruelty are common in this world and we become easily blinded to what's always there. Bliss does not necessarily translate into the visible world. Personally, I don't care what happens to me; only consciousness of Divinity—for lack of a better word—has any meaning. This is not a high or a legal drug—far from it. Serenity, love, and compassion result when we truly abandon resistance to what is, without self-serving reasons and unconscious ego demands for control, manipulation, and survival carried to the relationship level. I'd rather be sick, alone, and abandoned by the world having that essence flow through this carcass than having all the riches and good fortune in the world. Whatever good thing happens is just a bonus for which I'm humbly grateful.

Individual mystical experience is not the end. While it may shake us to our very core and result in the abandoning of our safety nets, we must always return to the marketplace and integrate it into our daily lives for as long as the body lives.

Piety and heroic deeds do not necessarily constitute holiness. The holy ones are those who become transparent to God—those in whom the Divine has broken through.

WILD GNOSIS...

*S*ince as early as I can remember—since before I could speak—I have been carried in the flow of a Love and an all-encompassing sense of Presence that I call "Mystery," because no name can contain it. It is first-hand experience, and I find resonance in the poetry of mystics and in the words of some of the early and modern Gnostics. That was only the beginning of a never-ending mystical journey. I'm not religious in any conventional way, and possibly not at all. Instead, I'm a free-thinker and a mystic. By mystic I mean the direct experience of the Extraordinary, without names or definition. I have coined the term "Wild Gnosis" to describe my approach.

In the 1970's I coined the term "Wild Gnosis" to differentiate it from "Gnosticism," another "ism." Since then, many people *erroneously* thinking that they understand what it means have tried to define it in their own words, always missing the mark. I'll try again, but remember, words are symbols and not the thing itself. "Wild Gnosis can approximately be described as a direct, transforming experience left untamed and unconditioned by cultural and socio-religious beliefs; the state prior to thought and the interpretation of the experience, unconfined by concepts and images. Awareness of Wild Gnosis arises in a quiet mind, in a dimension not touched by chronological time. We find it when we are fully in the present. Not before and not later, but here and now."

You who ask me to show you the way: Neti neti. Nothing. Nada. Nada, the word that St. John of the Cross uses to describe his teaching in its entirety. Neti neti, the Sanskrit word in Advaita Vedanta that means "not this, not that," or "neither this, nor that." This is apophasis and the way of the Gnostic Sanctuary. This is our way, our path, our Tao. Wild Gnosis.

I speak of Wild Gnosis. By "wild" I mean gnosis left untamed, impossible to cage with concepts or explanations. It stands on its own. Explanations and expansions only add bars to an empty cage. Two widely different things must be kept in mind by those seeking gnosis. One, there is the actual gnosis—direct, first-hand, permanent lightning strike that changes every previous knowing. Second, the many interpretations of gnosis and views of what it actually means. The first is gnosis. The second is just hearsay, even when truthful, whether uttered by contemporary people or by those who died long ago.

Wild Gnosis comes to us as the untamable love relationship with the Divine that cannot be confined by dictates, definitions, concepts, cultural conditioning, and traditional religion.

When we are truly present, which is in eternity, which is in gnosis, which has no time to make a cage of concepts and dissect and kill the moment (because it is beyond thought and time) we find sacredness in the moment everywhere.

What I wrote is not just something I say, but something I live and practice and have done so consistently for nearly five decades. I use the term "gnosis" in its Greek meaning and not to denote adherence to any particular texts or religion, therefore I reserve to myself the freedom to highlight the texts of any tradition in which I recognize this gnosis. I think that we are hardwired for gnosis, but that we are so conditioned by our beliefs and culture that few pass beyond beliefs and concepts. Mine is *not* the gnosis of dualism, elitism, and separatism, but the gnosis of mystical union that knows no frontiers.

Some would argue that it is the brain that creates the gnostic experience; however, it does not do so, in the same manner that it does not create physical reality, although it creates its evaluation and judgment of that reality. The human brain processes and interprets physical reality according to its makeup and our individual filters. The familiar brain tries to do the same with gnosis, but when it makes the attempt (and it does that automatically) it is no longer gnosis, but a caricature, an interpretation of something, because it is unable to capture it. That's why I coined the term "wild gnosis," meaning something that remains wild and untamed by our familiar brain and by our experiences and conditioning.

Let us for a moment forget about all these concepts such as truth, virtue, resurrection, and even gnosis. We can only talk about them when we are separate from them. Let us enter into a sacred space within. Not one that I tell you, or that the old Gnostics tell you. Not a vertical place you have to reach, not a horizontal one, but a different one, one that has never been thought before. This is a place you have known since infancy; before you heard of God and commandments; without pictures in your mind; without goals or a place to reach; without debt or karma—a new place of freedom with no past and with no expectation; a place where you can stop and take a deep breath. Breathe deeply now and reach through a gateway within your Being, through the root of your soul, beyond your name and identity: a place of total trust and safety. Breathe and extend your soul. Breathe slowly and deeply and prepare for the celebration of the mystery.

SANCTUARY...

*I*n May 1978 the feast of Pentecost appeared with blinding revelation as the time to open this cycle. There was opposition to that date in finding a location on that day, but the date relentlessly pursued me, with a persistence that could not be denied. I didn't know where and how, but we had to do it in a public place, not at anyone's home and not at any other time. It burned in my mind and consented to no compromise. Finally I just let go and said, "I have done my human part to the degree I'm able. I have run out of ideas, for almost everywhere I called was available on other dates, but this is the one you want. It is your turn now. If you want it so, then you'll have to do it. The next morning I received a call from the Presbyterian Church in Palo Alto that the rental of their chapel had just been canceled and that, if I still wanted it, it was mine. That chapel had been my first choice. What I didn't notice is that on that year Pentecost and Mother's Day fell on the same date, that's why so many places were booked for special services. What an interesting coincidence! Here is the Holy Spirit as Divine Mother, revealing her work in this cycle and pushing for the day when we honor the Mother.

Since early childhood I had already dedicated myself to the work I do today, even though I didn't expect that I would ever form a church. For mine has been a life of overlapping mystical experience and everyday reality, without ever finding a conflict or separation between the two. I see no conflict in completely embracing my humanity, including human love, pushing the barriers of what society expects, and good belly laughs without pretense. How can one not? I ask for I know not how to live any other way. Divinity's voice comes across very loudly when you dwell in the desert. And dwelling in the desert I did—and still do. Like the Shekinah, I have always remained a foreigner, an exile, wherever I have gone. I add to that self-sense of otherworldliness in that I purposely avoid speaking any language like the natives of wherever I find myself.

The Lovers of God can meet anywhere, whether at a park, a private house, a cafe or a restaurant. External sounds become background music coming as if from a distant dimension. Any place can be our temple, where the aliveness of the moment transforms all things. Even after having a temple space for many years, I have always continued to practice a form of nomadic spirituality.

It was an imperative and a never-ending calling from beyond the stars that drove me to create the physical Gnostic Sanctuary (Ecclesia Gnostica Mysteriorum) in 1978. This is a body created as a sovereign state for Divinity to transmit Its Ineffable Presence in this world. It knows no limits and demands no conditions, keeping no ledgers on what and how much I give and never expecting anything to come back to me. Nevertheless, incredible blessings never cease. That Presence of the Extraordinary never reveals Itself as a Father or Mother, but in a more blended and intimate manner as lover and Beloved and this is reflected in our Gnostic Sanctuary Eucharist ritual.

Religious texts and myths offer us a multilayered picture, a poetic work of art that can point us beyond a three-dimensional world into the Mysteries of Being and into our role in this co-salvific drama being played out in the cosmos. When we interpret them literally, focusing on the characters in the story rather than on their meaning and teaching, we make idols out of them, and thus neutralize their power.

When I founded the Sanctuary in 1978, I envisioned a place that I would like to attend, with no membership, beliefs, or dogma—a refuge for spiritual travelers, where no one would impose their reality upon another. Today, it is still a Sanctuary for travelers, for passersby. To be a passerby we need to drop our personal agendas, even our religious ones, and our hopes and expectations for a certain result. From such a mind comes generosity without thinking that we are giving; courage without thinking that we are brave; full acceptance and embracing without thinking we are tolerant; wisdom without thinking that we know best or needing to change anyone else; transformation without thinking that we are changing; freedom regardless of outward circumstances.

Meditation and prayer at the Gnostic Sanctuary necessitates a letting go, a surrendering to the moment just as it is. Once the struggle ceases, thought slows down, and sacred silence comes in. In this silence the dimension of the extraordinary can flow through, for it has always been there, but sometimes we don't perceive it when we have just been too busy thinking and struggling. Stop now, rest, and let Divinity emanate from and through your hidden chambers and fill your being.

Our physical Gnostic Sanctuary, in Redwood City, California, is an outpost for the Pleroma, a Sanctuary for Travelers. Its function can be described, but its essence cannot—it must be experienced. At one level, it is a physical sacred space that evokes profound peace and facilitates deep communion with the Mystery that is within and without. At another level it is not a physical place at all, but rather a portal, a gateway that exists simultaneously within temporal space and time as well as eternity. It is also a rich archetypal symbol layered with meaning. It is an inclusive sacred space with no doctrine or dogma that welcomes seekers from all traditions, backgrounds, and beliefs. We have no membership, have no jurisdictions and are not affiliated with any other body, and there are no barriers based on one's sexual orientation, gender, or ethnicity.

In seeing through the ruses of this world, it is not our illusion of a personal self that we liberate. Through a flash of anamnesis, the divine Spark breaks free of its chains. "Gather all my limbs which, since the foundation of the world, have been scattered abroad in this aeon, and reunite them together and receive them into the Light!" (From the Book of the Great Logos, as quoted in the Gnostic Sanctuary Eucharist ritual).

There is a treasure at the core of every metaphor. Even when read at the lowest level, there's still an entertaining and even inspiring story hinting at us, inviting us to discover that there is something deeper concealed within it and that becomes revealed to those with eyes to see and ears to hear. A good text deserves to be unwrapped and understood in all its different layers, levels, and nuances, but the intellect does not take us far enough. It barely covers the surface. It is when reason fails and we stand powerless, in total surrender in the face of the unimaginable, that the doors to *pneuma* open and the real adventure begins. Then we hold the key. We do not read the text, but enter the Source that gave rise to it.

It is my hope that all those I train to the priesthood reach that state of commitment from within and not superimposed from outside before ordination, and that they are indeed Juliet to the Romeo that we call metaphorically *the ineffable God* or the *God beyond God*.

Once and for all: I'm not about teaching people Gnostic tradition, Mary Magdalene tradition, or any other kind of tradition. What I'm about is awakening those ready to wake up. That is the essence of Gnosis. I'm constantly being asked why, when I have been initiated in the Mary Magdalene tradition or the Gnostic tradition, I don't talk about any kind of historical or scriptural interpretation; why I don't argue or even discuss in favor or against any historical version or interpretation of teachings. I'll tell you why: Whether it is Christianity, Gnosticism, Mary Magdalene, or practices to "attain" something, almost everyone uses those pointers and practices as means of entertainment, distractions so they can dream that they are awake and not see who they are and the plight they are in. I'm not about wasting my time and yours on another crutch, another game to keep the dark away. The Gnostic Sanctuary is not another "spiritual" entertainment center.

Symbols and metaphors, like words, are a type of language that mean and stand for something. They can heal and they can hurt. Like words, definitions, translations, and definitive interpretations are not nearly enough. Often, they tend to divide rather than clarify. Like with dancing and music, one must have a feel for them; a knack that cannot be taught, but that can be acquired, where rules do not always apply.

Someone asked elsewhere about where the soul goes after death. While I don't give definite answers, and think it is useless to speculate, I'd like to present one possible way of looking at this: The body lives surrounded and inter-penetrated by soul; hence it is ensouled as in soul acquiring a body and not as in a body having a soul. Soul goes where it has always remained prior, during, and after Body. When the physical body (a space suit needed to function in this planet and dimension) is too dented and no longer usable or needed, Body is discarded. Post-death visitations may be seen as contacting traveling companions still serving their tour of duty on earth.

MARY MAGDALENE...

*J*n January 1962 I was presented with something that eyes had seen and ears had heard by a very small group, but that the world had not known outside that little group. It was something that, for me, was extraordinary while it was, simultaneously, very familiar. That was when I was contacted for the first time by the Holy Order of Miriam of Magdala. This Order had as its only purpose to preserve Miriam's teachings in the same manner that I have been passing them on here every Sunday for those who have ears to hear.

How can I present you, my Magdalene? How can I awaken you, who speak in the blood of all? While the world keeps you asleep, chaos reigns. How can I present you, so that they who hear my voice will rise from their slumber and say: enough! The moment is now! You who transcend history and live in the hearts of those who seek you: How can I praise you, O mother mine who never bore children but who eternally gives birth and nurture all who dare rest upon your breast?

And the Magdalene answers: My message is written in

forms of flesh and blood, in forms of feather, scale, sap, cloud, and dust. But don't worship me. Do not define me by religious and worldly standards. I am Isis, Shekinah, Sophia. I'm Miriam, reborn in your flesh each time you call my name. Do not worship me. Do not define me. I have come to remind you of who you are, beyond all appearances. I have come to awaken love and humility in the midst of chaos and strife. I have no religion. I teach no religion. I belong to no religion. All I know is Infinite Love, and this Love is knocking at the gates of your heart, trapped within, shouting for freedom. Like rushing waters and unstoppable, forceful winds, love assails the dams that the world has built around you, breaking through your defenses, tumbling the walls built around you. Fear not.

Open the gates in trust and innocence. Let Love flow through you. Love moves of its own authority and does not belong to you, and it does not belong to me. Like life, it comes from the source of all. Let your heart open, leave all judgments, assumptions, and expectations behind. Throw your doors open.

Listen—love is knocking. Silence—remain silent. Come to love's awesome living presence. Come into my embrace; come into love beyond all imaginings. Come, you have paid your price. The moment is now. Let me anoint your feet and pour balsam upon your crown.

Almost every year I present to you the deeper, spiritual aspects of Mary Magdalene, as she appears as Holy Shekinah, anima mundi, or world soul, and as teacher, transmitting the power of the Holy Spirit. She also demonstrates in her own journey the means to attain liberation from what enslaves and torments us —men and women—not from the outside, but from the nature of this planet from which we are composed.

This year was not very different from the ones before, so I wrote a talk concentrating on this last one. Then I deleted seven pages of what was a very good and comprehensive talk, in my opinion. After that, I wrote ten pages that I liked even more, as it comprised a compendium of history and symbol that blended in a most harmonious way. I deleted that one too, for I'm not presenting Mary Magdalene to an audience of the unwashed, but to a group of people who already have heard her call and have responded accordingly in their hearts.

Finally, I had to stop and cried to her in frustration, "What do you want of me?" "You are not very easy to please this year, are you?"

Finally her answer emerged, which surprised me, for it was the theme I presented in the voice of the Jesus of the Gospels on Maundy Thursday when Jesus asked his disciples, "Do you understand what it is that I have done to you?" So I asked her, "Are you asking me what it is that you have done to me? No wonder you appear as Christ-Sophia, for you ask the same questions."

Whether the Magdalene and Yeshua married or not is wholly irrelevant to the Mystery of the Bridal Chamber. It is not earthly marriage, but the male and female aspects of God and of the inner and the outer that must be reunited in us. Paraphrasing the words of St. John of the Cross who wrote of this cosmic union, "Oh night that guided me, Oh, night more lovely than the dawn, Oh, night that joined Beloved with lover, Lover transformed in the Beloved."

Our Mary Magdalene tradition is a teacher-led tradition, like Zen Buddhism, and not a Master-of-Divinity tradition. It is one that leads beyond intellectual belief to the gnosis that Divinity resides not only all around us, but within our own bodies. It is actually a direct Divinity-to-person contact and communication. I feel a fierce responsibility with each transmission that those I ordain will not just be ordained in ritual or in name, but that the initiation will resonate throughout all the worlds.

Approximately two thousand years ago, a woman was born carrying within herself the seeds that, in blossoming, would transform her mortal flesh into an embodiment of She whom sages call "the hidden mystery" and "She who remains with us." She is the same who bore the names and titles of Hokmah, Isis, Shekinah, Sophia, Aphrodite, Holy Wisdom, the Hidden Mother. Her name was Miriam, later said of Magdala.

You can reach her at that holy sanctuary without external prerequisites. You can do it anywhere, under any conditions, in a noisy restaurant or in an ashram, amidst the chaos of the world or in a beautiful retreat in the mountains. She is not dependent on outside surroundings. She lives in the anchorite and the urban mystic. We find Her surrounded by barbed wire as well as surrounded by gorgeous foliage and waterfalls. Her voice speaks through the ages, since before the beginning of time: "I am here, now, anywhere and at any time."

Miriam…O Miriam… When did we first fall in love with you? When did our heart first resonate to your name? Was it when you sat at the feet of Jesus, enraptured by his word, in communion beyond sound and time, when the teaching and you became one? Or was it when you met him at the empty tomb and fell at his feet calling him, *Rabbuni!?* Perhaps, I think, it was the first time we heard your name… It was the time when we knew your story was our story; that we were there with you, in you, anointing his feet, drying them with our hair; walking in the streets of Galilee. Was that the time in which we knew your story was our story? When did we become skins to bear your name?

She certainly was a woman not held by the conventions, roles, and expectations of her time: maligned, rejected by her own companions—the apostles—and misunderstood by most. Who is she? She is the one we think she is: virgin, whore, apostle, bride. But the nature of a being can only be known when we have left ourselves behind. This knowledge is not knowledge of the head, but of the heart. It is what mystics call experience, a divine knowing. It is gnosis when all "isms" are left behind.

Going back, while Jesus was still in the flesh, the exorcism of the seven demons he performed on Mary eloquently conveys to us Mary Magdalene's exalted status. They represent the seven layers of reality in the cosmology of the early Gnostics describing the path of enlightenment: liberation from the seven archons or false gods, freedom from the power of ignorance. Through this story, the ancient Gnostics recognized her as one of their own.

She portrays the very nature of enlightenment. She is liberated, not resigned. She faces reality. She unmasks the Powers of Wrath that still see separation, a world out there apart from each individual. Her liberation comes not from succumbing under the rules of the universe, but from seeing that there's no separate person to give in and no separate, overwhelming universe to give in to.

Mary Magdalene, Maria Magdalena, Miriam of Magdala, to whom we have dedicated our shrine, is the woman of story and myth. She lives—always—beyond time, forever mysterious and revealing. She is always beckoning and alluring, enticing us to follow her into the mysterious and forbidden.

Miriam of Magdala's image embodies the lost Sophia, the hidden and forgotten soul of humanity. Shrouded in darkness and neglect, she appears—often feared and rejected, yet always beckoning, seductive and dangerous at times, as the call of the Spirit often is.

Shifting this story to the highest, pneumatic level, it explodes with ecstasy and spiritual understanding. Mary Magdalene is revealed as the Bride of Christ, a mirror of our soul, where the male and the female are restored as a single one. She is the revealer of the mysteries concealed, the One who knew the All, and their union fulfills the completion and restoration of the Divine mystery. Their story is our story, as it has always been and ever shall be. But then, these are only words, words are not the experience, and belief in any of this won't make us pneumatic unless we awaken in an eternal present. The mystic experience and the experience of gnosis are one and the same. They are just the beginning for a world beyond imaginings.

The story of the Magdalene becomes our history: The history of our androgynous soul, of the male and female journey; the timeless history of our soul, a blueprint of wholeness and restoration.

At the symbolic level there is more than one truth: first, the history of womankind is retold in the many stories of Mary Magdalene, who embodies a new restored woman; an archetype breaking the chains that restrained, enslaved, and oppressed her feminine power. In this same manner, she also embodies aspects of the Holy Sophia and those of several different goddesses, vying for justice and renewal in an all-too-unbalanced and unjust patriarchal history, whose grip still strangles women in many countries and religions to this day.

SOPHIA...

Sitting with my latte at Douce France in Palo Alto, CA, I looked out the window. A small round man past his fifties, unshaven, and reminiscent of a sparrow walked by.

She rose in me and filled me with compassion. And Her voice silently spoke—not through my ears, but through every cell:

"These are my children." My eyes moved to the tables in front and around me, watching the people so seriously intent in their conversations, so oblivious to the Presence observing them through my eyes. "These are my children and I love them all. I draw them to me. I dry their tears and smile at their laughter. I calm their fears, but they hear me not. These are my children, exiled in a labor of love whose purpose they have forgotten. Now they are lost, standing and judging from their self-conceived moral ground, disguising their fears with words they think are wise. But soon they'll return to me. They don't know that I'm never separate from them even though they are ignorant of me.

"Sometimes I reach them at night, in their deepest dreams. Or when they dream awake, forgetting the next second what they learned in me.

"These are my children and I remain with them without end."

She persisted, looking through my eyes and feeling through my heart—silent now, but in total possession of my being. There is no I, no history, no past, no identity: Only She.

I partially emerge from this melding to turn on my laptop and write these words. I say "She," although there is no indication of gender. Sometimes it is He, but this time it is undeniably She: the loving, soothing, all patient and wise She.

In the depths of the abyss, we find the fountainhead and matrix of Sophia, pregnant with infinite possibilities. Divinity pours Its life through her. In her womb, Wisdom-Sophia carries the blueprint of all prototypes before matter ever came into being. She remains with us in our exile, for she is the tender mother of mercy and great redeemer. She is the beginning and she is the end.

Human-created systems distort truth by ignorance or design and relentlessly hunger to rule all minds in the outer world. Invisible, moving through mental smog and confusion, the Holy Sophia carves her dwelling place. She paves from within a path out of darkness, and banishing illusion, She marks the Way, igniting the mind with Her Light. Ignored and rejected by the onslaughts from the bottomless bag of tricks of the Archons, She moves swiftly, as the risks are great for those who have seen what Her light reveals. And so is the journey of the Gnostic, bringing light in the midst of darkness and illuminating every place where he or she stands. Indelibly branded by the Seal of the World Straddlers, they recognize each other as knights and fellow Travelers, united in Holy Company throughout this journey during the night. With friendship and Holy Company to help illumine the period of voluntary exile from our True Home, how can it be exile?

At each inhalation we breathe in the Holy Spirit, as our earth suits did when they took their first breath and became a living soul. Let us consciously return the favor. As we exhale, with each exhalation, let us breathe out into the world the fire of life, flooding with the Holy Spirit the holy sparks lost and asleep within the heart of matter. Let us awaken and reunite the fragmented limbs of a God calling out to us in yearning through every existing thing.

In this age of Sophia, the path has no place for saviors and personality worship. A responsible guide refuses deification, while the spiritual direction offered to seekers can only help reveal the obstacles that prevent Divinity from fully awakening. The ego appears as it is, as if the world has lifted its mask, and the soul remains without illusion or pretense, in awe and great humility.

Today I was asked about Ialdabaoth, for I rarely think of this mythological character except when I personalize principles in writing teaching stories: Chief Archon and creator, implementer and preserver of thinking patterns and of restrictive social, political, and religious belief systems and other systems of metaphor that control through judgment, shame, and fear. Although those systems seem to change, they just alter their names and rearrange their pieces, for they remain thoughts of the same thinker. The spectrum of the dream oscillates from the pleasant to the unbearable as long as no one awakens. Awaken, and the binding chains are broken. The thinker and the thought are seen for what they are. The game is up. Sophia's veils have fallen.

Since I first heard the term "Holy Spirit," I had always sensed a flavor of wisdom and femininity. I equated that Holy Spirit with the bride of the Song of Songs. For me that was never just a poem between lovers, although it can be seen that way too, but a poem that opens wide the doors of the heart.

It is possible to restore the awareness of the Divine to our daily lives that has been lost to intellect and spiritual life. That's the meaning of bringing the feminine. What we call "the feminine principle" is the realm of intuition, insight, and inclusivity. It is also caring, awareness, compassion, and love. The feminine principle is the bridge between I and we. Men and women are both heirs to this principle.

We have deeply imprinted within us the image of this nurturing, loving, all-protecting mother and lover-mistress, calling us with a sweet voice, with her arms open to embrace us as we dissolve in tears. Hers is also the image of the Divine Lover, She whom every person hopes to see in the eyes of His beloved, but that no human can satisfy, except those in whom the Shekinah reposes.

There is a legend that when Mohammad Ali first opened the jar containing the Gnostic codices in 1945, a cloud of golden dust rose into the air and dissipated into the atmosphere. Whether you call this event coincidence or synchronicity, it vividly fixes itself within our psyches as a great treasure being suddenly released in the deep awareness of our culture. Images of the feminine principle rise as Sophia, as if a genie had been freed from its bottle to never be confined again.

The purpose of the union of opposites, that incredible attraction of polarities that we celebrate in the Eucharist and the myths, are only outer plays of the real union, the real Bridal Chamber that is the reunion of all the parts of our being and without projecting it outside, where the energy dissipates. There is the sacred bride and the Divine lover. They are not just archetypes of ideas that may leave us breathless with their love and desire for each other. They move us so because it is the call of the Divine God within us, calling us, guiding us by his voice, for we have gone astray.

So, there exists within us a divine spark, a beautiful pearl, unsullied, undefiled by the world and the chaos of matter. This is the priceless pearl, the light of the Spirit, which is itself the source of our own longing for the Divine Presence.

So may the grace of the one who is full of grace dwell with us and lead us into the Light, that we may find the redeeming power of Sophia within us, where we might put her on as a "robe of honor" and put her about us as a "crown of joy."

The story of Sophia is not just a philosophical conundrum or a moral tale. Sophia is the bringing back of the feminine image of the redeemed redeemer, which restores the hero in all of us. We all have within us, regardless of our gender, the potential to be noble knights in service to Our Lady Sophia; we are all, male or female, prepared as a bride to receive the Bridegroom, our true royal Selfhood, the Christ within.

WORDS...

Words, words, words! What good are words when they only drown your voice? You speak to us in the silence. Silence not only of sounds, but silence of thought. We need words to aid others in not giving up, to point toward the discovery that You are there and can be heard if only we stop all that pretentious movement; if only we let go of what books and others have said about you; if only we stop telling others what you are and assist in their hearing you directly rather than having a secondhand relationship with you (which is no relationship at all). For You, unexplainable You, are the only teacher and companion of our souls.

Semantics play a powerful role in communication, especially words that have different meanings. Take for instance, the words "mystic" or "gnostic," or that trickiest of all words: "truth." People often appear to be disagreeing when they are using diverging definitions of the same word when, in fact, there is no disagreement, just two different conversations. We must never assume that the other is using the same definition as ours before adding our two-cents worth lest we unwittingly equivocate. That someone does not understand or disagrees with something doesn't automatically make that something wrong. Just because someone is uncomfortable with something doesn't necessarily make that something wrong. Ultimately, it is not what someone does or says to us that matters. What matters is how we respond, what we do and what we say.

Symbols and metaphors, like words, are a type of language that mean and stand for something. They can heal and they can hurt. Like words, definitions, translations, and definitive interpretations are not nearly enough. Often, they tend to divide rather than clarify. Like with dancing and music, one must have a feel for them; a knack that cannot be taught, but can be acquired, where rules do not always apply. I frequently observe how some people tend to re-state what I say in their own words, thus making it appear as if they were correcting what I said or making a comment as if they were responding to something that I never said. They not only hijack what I wrote, but mislead other readers, and more often than not, bleed the life out of my original statement.

Human beings are story-making animals. We do so constantly, even in our sleep while we dream. We communicate by telling each other stories. These seem to help in processing our perceptions of reality. The more outlandish and unfamiliar the story, the deeper its source as it emerges from our unconscious, the more beneficial it is in stretching the mind. Thus, we keep our imagination flexible and fluid lest it becomes calcified by the inability of considering more than one system of metaphors. Fortunately, there are many models of reality for us to play with and visionaries, poets, artists, and scientists continue to enrich us with new ones all the time.

There is a dark side to stories and that is when people believe the story as fact and become possessed by their archetypes. Some of the darkest periods in human history have come into existence because of the interpretation given to a story. There are no bad stories. There are only people that process them through their unacknowledged, unredeemed shadow and use them to visit their projections on others. They see them as mandates to commit atrocities. Their dream becomes a nightmare for others, sometimes for millions. People create fictions about whole groups of people and even animals. You don't even have to read about the Inquisition, witches burning, and the influence that Wagner's work had on Hitler. Just read the conspiracy theories du jour. On the upside, stories can effect meaningful changes in the psyche and have done much to inspire people, encourage them, and to bring out the best in humanity.

Once the story is told no one can control its destiny. It belongs to the minds of the hearers who will interpret it through their filters. Every story may potentially possess the hearer and they still do. We cannot ensure that it will be understood properly, even if the words are passed intact, which is not possible, because the words have different nuances of meaning for each hearer and the words also change meaning as the language evolves. However, that's not a bad thing. The story evolves. Reading through the Old Testament we find an evolving God that moves from warrior to lawgiver to judge to being synonymous with love. Everything can swing either way. It does not depend on the story but on the individual who hears it, and the hearers create their own derivation of the story.

In the Gospel of Philip, it is said: "Truth did not come into the world naked, but came in form and images, for otherwise the world would not accept her." We use words and images as symbols in the same manner that our dreams appear in shapes and forms, for that's how our human minds process reality. These forms stand for and direct us to something beyond definition and qualities that must be penetrated directly. Words, poor as they are and sparingly as we must use them, act as conveyances for catapulting hearers to their unimagined meaning before abandoning them at the threshold of Reality. That's one of the mysteries of gnosis, which ceases to be a mystery through gnosis.

Our human brains don't rest until they find answers (albeit flawed and temporary) to the phenomenon of existence and its myriad psychological implications. We are also creative. We make stories in order to make sense of our perceived realities, whether those stories bear any relation to facts or not, as long as the brain feels that it has made some sense of it all. Perhaps that's why we make a creator god in our own image. That god may be as good and compassionate as we are; or as vengeful, cruel, jealous, and envious as humans can be. The worst part is that we worship and serve our creations.

I'm not saying that there is not an uncreated Source, but that Source can't be seen and much less described through ordinary consciousness. Anything said in words can only point to something that a hearer may or may not even intuit. Of that Source, we can only speak apophatically, by saying what is not. Perhaps that's what the commandment, "Thou shalt have no other gods before me and Thou shalt not bow nor worship them" means. We create gods in our own image and we worship our creations. Is God good or evil? That often depends on whether we just won the lottery or on whether we have just lost everything we cared about, including health and freedom. No wonder Yeshua taught not to make treasures on earth where everything is corruptible and perishable.

When we realize all the games we play to keep the dark away, how we use and have been used by thought, we finally wake up to who we are and the nature of our role on this planet. Not only do we become plugged into a prior Source, but we are able to unwrap the gnosis of a destiny we have always known but didn't know we knew.

Thought has its place at the level in which it works best. There, it is essential and the better the thinker, the better the job. But we try to find the unthinkable through thought and the intellect. At the level of pneuma where one finds gnosis, thought doesn't reach. It makes stories about what it imagines the Sought is, and those thoughts can even hold and produce emotional content that can powerfully affect the psyche and the life of a person. When it deals with mythology and beliefs it is often mistaken for gnosis, but it bears no relation to it. Even psychic and paranormal experiences have nothing to do with the mystical experience of something I'll call "the Encounter with Source (or Presence)."

When the individual continues on the quest without stopping at the satisfying story, something else that is un-thought and un-catchable by thought appears. St. John of the Cross, in his masterpiece "The Spiritual Canticle," writes about seeking the Beloved, which is the term he and other mystics before and after him have used. That Beloved relentlessly draws and haunts him. He writes, "Seeking my love I will go over mountains and meadows, traversing frontiers. Neither will I pick the flowers nor will I fear the wild beasts." We can call the encounter with the unconscious and the unredeemed self "the wild beasts." The flowers are the luminous, delicious, deceiving candies that we find on the way. They are pleasurable, but like most candies, they just make you fat—they make the ego fat.

Used wisely, words can lead to beauty and understanding. Words can be sublime. I can even taste them as they roll off my tongue in poetry or a well-turned-out sentence. They stand as avatars for meaning and intent. They hint and tease us. They can dance us to the terminal. Once there, we leave the words as if they were trains, abandon the station, and enter Meaning, for words act as messengers that may lead us to the sender, but the sender remains above and beyond, while still remaining concealed within words. At the same time, words also most often tend to mislead, for much of what is understood in an instant tends to get lost in terms and sentences. No wonder there are so many religions claiming the same Source. The story of the Tower of Babel meant to reach heaven warns us of verbosity, of the confusion of language used unwisely. The text from the Gospel of Philip reminds and warns us of the story of the Tower of Babel meant to reach heaven, but instead the confusion of the language took place.

People tend to interpret what they see based on their background: A Hindu describes a Hindu god, an atheist doesn't see a Hindu god or a Christian god, but some being. Different cultures see the same thing, but their interpretation depends on what they believe. We believe what we see, but what we see depends on what we believe.

Religious texts and myths offer us a multilayered picture, a poetic work of art that can point us beyond a three-dimensional world into the Mysteries of Being and into our role in this co-salvific drama being played out in the cosmos. When we interpret them literally, focusing on the characters in the story rather than on their meanings and teachings, we make idols out of them, and thus neutralize their power. Messages and clues are all around us, but humans tend to focus on the messengers rather than the message. It is easier to worship a figure of light than it is to unwrap what the story is telling us and what this figure stands for and is showing us. This is something that we must see and experience for ourselves, for we can only know what we experience directly and not by what another person tells us, or by their interpretation. This is different than receiving guidance to the Source, which becomes essential at a certain point if one is not to be derailed by illusions.

There is a treasure at the core of every metaphor. Even when read at the lowest level, there's still an entertaining and even inspiring story hinting at us, inviting us to discover that something deeper concealed within it and that becomes revealed to those with eyes to see and ears to hear. A good text deserves to be unwrapped and understood in all its different layers, levels, and nuances, but the intellect does not take us far enough. It barely covers the surface. It is when reason fails and we stand powerless, in total surrender in the face of the unimaginable, that the doors to pneuma open and the Real adventure begins. Then we hold the key. We do not read the text, but enter the Source that gave rise to it.

I write in story form what is derived from the experience. The different types of stories are like speaking in different languages that I know fluently. Yeshua used similar methods when using stories about fishermen, master and overseer, shepherds, rich man/poor man, and others. "The kingdom of God is like..." He'll compare it to something else because the kingdom of God cannot be put into words. A gnostic doesn't take the narratives literally, but as myth pointing to a Reality greater than actual history. That doesn't mean that Yeshua didn't exist, but that whether he existed or not doesn't take away from what he stands for. Gnosis is not based on belief but on direct experience. It doesn't matter what is believed. The mind allows many types of worldviews. As I wrote elsewhere, "Throughout it all there is a running current, a linking and uniting thread, telling you in stories and word pictures what words cannot convey directly and what cannot be passed on to another, but what an interior but insistent part of the reader knows, finds familiar, and recognizes. If you read all that I say and there is no inner response, or if you give my words a literal, concrete, world-factual interpretation, then we are not speaking the same language and it is best to just pass me by.

SILENCE...

Sacred emptiness and silence came visiting tonight. Silence for those who suffer illness, fear, and loss. Silence for the dead. Silence for the animals.

Silence for all who love me. Silence for those who do not wish me well. Silence for the stranger. Silence for our sakes. Forgiveness without end.

Entering the "space" as I write these last words for tonight; breathing and staying within the gap between the words, between the sentences, between chords, empty of thought, without name, without definition of self.

Entering into these always unexpected—but often encountered —moments of ecstasy. These are recognized by their numinous beauty as sacraments—leakages from beyond the veil overlapping into this world of form.

Listen in inner silence. That awesome power is calling you and waiting for you. At first, its voice may not be discernible, with all the voices of the world demanding your attention. Do not block those. Acknowledge them and you'll recognize them for what they are. Listen deeper, beyond their cacophony, without expectations. We were not taught to listen in the silence, so the neglected organs of inner hearing (ears to hear) may take a bit to be heard at first.

Some fear the darkness and the void, but it is in the vastness of emptiness that fullness dwells, and where darkness is nothing but unutterable radiance.

As we return from having been into a field beyond thought and identity the whole of life becomes a sacrament. Even the most mundane thing turns into the bread and water of life.

At that first moment that is not a moment, before the moment begins, there is silence. Can we remain with it, without thought and words, without intercepting and hijacking it with comparisons, labels, or concepts? Can you cross the threshold of the Unknown as the gates to wild gnosis open wide and reveal its Mysteries to you?

My meditation is not a means to an end. There is no end, no arrival. I enter through time, but it's entirely out of time. It's not to receive new thoughts, ideas, or concepts or a new road or pilgrimage; not expecting anything to happen; not seeking or collecting knowledge—but abandoning all this. It is silence, naked and without disguises. There I know why I'm here. I can only move accordingly.

The keynote emphasizing the universal constant that reveals our underlying unity proves the same now as it ever was millennia ago: the phenomenon of waking consciousness is always and everywhere the same. It is universal and spans all ages and traditions. It does not matter what holy names, if any, we invoke; it does not matter what liturgies we use or what beliefs we have. It remains a universal unifying constant underlying this mixture of apparently disparate and opposing elements. We are drawn together to reveal that the movement toward the One is an inexorable one: bright, incandescent, and transforming. Behind all these words and doings, there is a sacred emptiness in which God, if I may use that term as symbol, flows like a rushing river. It is in that emptiness that I feel totally fulfilled. It is the ending of me.

Let's not mistake emptiness with absolute nullity, for emptiness is the dwelling place of "infinite possibilities," a phrase that some of you have heard me use for decades. To create something new, we have to dig deeply into total Emptiness. Creating from what already exists is just reshaping patterns, as in a kaleidoscope, where at each turn the pieces of glass rearrange themselves, but there are only a limited number of pieces of glass and only re-creation is possible. The more the pieces, the more complex and beautiful the picture, but it is just the same old pieces. Please, stay with me here if you are willing. Dig deep beyond the known, pass the familiar. Go beyond such concepts as God, Time, Religion, Spirituality, Death, the Universe. Go beyond belief. All those concepts already follow a basic design. May we go beyond, perhaps to a point abuzz with unformed possibilities, uncreated and undesigned? Stay very still. You have just left time.

We return to everyday reality carrying no memory of a moment that cannot be called a moment, for it is beyond time. Untouched by thought or memory, but with senses atingle with knowledge beyond knowledge that always remains unknown, every living cell remains a witness to the extraordinary, even as they replicate themselves. We are forever branded with its flavor, haunted by its longing, peace, and forbidden knowledge, bearing Emptiness's unbearable secret. Some fear the darkness and the void, but it is in the vastness of emptiness that fullness dwells, and where darkness is nothing but unutterable radiance.

Unexpected moments of ecstasy act as spontaneous sacraments. They seep as leakages from the Source into this world of form.

By keeping quiet, repressing nothing, remaining attentive and by accepting reality—taking things as they are, and not as I want them to be—by doing all this, unusual knowledge has come to me, and unusual powers as well, such as I could never have imagined before. I always thought that when we accept things they overpowered us in some way or other. This turns out not to be true at all, and it is only by accepting them that one can assume an attitude toward them.

Surrender, go through the silent, secret ladder before we are noticed by control and time.

Begin by looking from the place of your inner silence, your stillness that sees and hears without judgment, without choosing or rejecting, just seeing everything pass, from listening to your breath, watching it, without directing it. It is already here. Don't combine yourself with any mode of time or any concept, or any conclusions to which you may have arrived, and immediately you will find yourself in a realm of neutrality, spaciousness, and silence. You shall become aware of Awareness.

Meditation this night ended in the same manner as my first voiced prayer as a small child when I first began to speak: "Don't ever let me forget."

Let your mind become quieter than the morning fog. Meet your Beloved who awaits within. Hush! Invite the silence and let your mind become still; as your body relaxes into infinity, your senses expand and become one with the world. A subtle luminosity, a serene radiance, a brilliantly transparent clarity shimmering as pure bright light explodes within your being. In your stead, only the luminous face of love and compassion remains, before whose radiance all images retreat, a Love so fierce it adoringly embraces both light and dark, both good and evil, both pleasure and pain without distinction, for it is beyond all dualities.

A PRAYER...

In my rejoicing, when the future looks safe and bright, you are with me. When disaster threatens to snap its jaws on me, you are with me. When my friends harden their hearts in my time of need, you are with me. In times of loss when all that is left is ashes, your Presence never leaves me. In my darkest hours, when your face seems closed and the future looms ominously like an endless pit, you are with me.

For you are with me and I am in you. I see you even when I can't see you. And when all I see is the dark of your face, a tunnel to unimaginable terrors, even through those terrors, even through those times, I am with you. For I love you in all you are and in all you give me, under any conditions, in your darkness and in your Light. For your darkness is brighter than the brightest visible light.

As a mother I hold you to my breast and as a lover I kiss your lips, and thus clasped together, in fear and in darkness, my senses begin to sing, aquiver in love and compassion, through the vortex of your terror and darkness, mixing and transforming, woven together, turning into an impossible embrace of unbearable joy and ecstasy without end.

For love unites us under any conditions in your darkness as well as your Light. For your darkness is brighter than the brightest visible or imagined brightness. In any manner of things we are never apart, for we are woven together. Give me your darkness, if that is your desire, and I will hold it until your ache and fragmentation turns into Wholeness and Light. Do with me what you will, but only according to your desire, not what the world desires. I cleave to you in my joy and I cleave to you in despair. I praise your name in love, trust, and blessing forevermore. Amen.

Some words about the above prayer: I wrote the first part of this prayer a year ago and the last part today. This is a portion of a conversation with the Divine Beloved, and not meant as poetry —for obviously it is not. The Beloved sometimes chooses to show me His brightest Light and most inebriating of smiles and, at other times, He comes as a mean drunk with thunder in His voice and storms in His eyes. They are not directed at me or, at least, I don't think so. I just happen to be there at some of those times and hear His voice and feel His need lashing from his wounded self. What else can I do but embrace Him, even if He acts like a cat that sometimes scratches and makes me bleed when He is in pain? Sometimes I think of Him as a vampire (probably in one of His disguises) who needs a little blood from time to time and I'm more than happy to let Him drink as much as He wants. He has a long history of showing this side of Himself to willing humans.

How can I speak of the Divine in such terms, you may ask? We are used to thinking of God as if he was Santa Claus, just there to give us things when we ask Him and get mad at Him when we don't get them. That's not my relationship with the

Divine. He knows what I need, and I know what It needs, when Divinity, manifesting through layers of density, appears insane when impressing senses manifesting in three-dimensional forms. Whatever our relationship, I have the best part of it. I just hope that He gets something out of it, too.

www.ingramcontent.com/pod-product-compliance
Lightning Source LLC
Chambersburg PA
CBHW031343160426
43196CB00007B/726